MAD FRANK'S
LONDON

MAD FRANK'S LONDON

Frankie Fraser
with James Morton

*For my four sons, Frank Jr, David, Patrick and Francis.
And my nephew, Jimmy.*

This paperback edition first published in 2002 by
Virgin Books Ltd
Thames Wharf Studios
Rainville Road
London W6 9HA

First published in hardback in Great Britain in 2001 by
Virgin Books Ltd

A catalogue record for this book is available from the British Library.

ISBN 0 7535 0714 5

Typeset by TW Typesetting, Plymouth, Devon

Printed and bound by Mackays of Chatham PLC

CONTENTS

PICTURE CREDITS

The author and publishers are grateful to the following sources for pictures reproduced in this book:

Draughtsman Ltd,   Maps, p. vii and p. viii
London W10
(Based on mapping generated by ERA-Maptec Ltd)

Illustrated section:

Hulton Getty   Jack 'Spot', p. 1;
                        George Blake, p. 2;
                        Ruth Ellis, p. 2;
                        The Messina brothers, p. 4;
                        Flower sellers, p. 5;
                        Harold Davidson, p. 6

Topham Picturepoint   The Krays, p. 1;
                        Mandy Rice-Davies, p. 3;
                        Billy Hill, p. 4

Author's own   Hampton Court Palace pub, p. 7;
                        The Castle Hotel, p. 8;
                        Marilyn/Frank/Renee and
                        Tommy Wisbey, p. 8

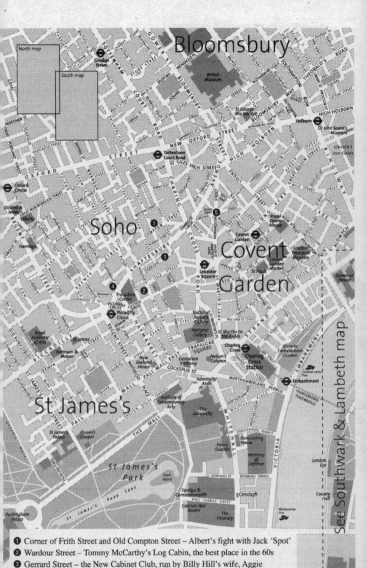

1. Corner of Frith Street and Old Compton Street – Albert's fight with Jack 'Spot'
2. Wardour Street – Tommy McCarthy's Log Cabin, the best place in the 60s
3. Gerrard Street – the New Cabinet Club, run by Billy Hill's wife, Aggie
4. Great Windmill Street – Jack Solomon's gym, where the faces hung out
5. Seven Dials – where Billy Hill was born

1. Cornwall Road – My birthplace (the building is now part of the station)
2. Blackfriars/ Union Street – the Ring as it was – now it's moved to the opposite side of the road
3. Walworth Road – my parents' flat, where we moved when I was five
4. Walworth Road – and just about opposite their flat was the Reform Club, which is how I came to join the Richardsons
5. Walworth Road/ Manor Place – Manor Place Baths, where we used to go to bathe
6. Lower Marsh – where I saw my first dead bodies

INTRODUCTION

You don't often find three stiffs when you do a screwing but that's what happened when Jimmy Essex, Dido Frett and me did a tailor's in Lower Marsh off the Waterloo Road in the war. They were the first dead people I ever saw. Dido and me had just got Jimmy out of Feltham Borstal. The wall wasn't that high, and we'd been to visit him so we knew exactly where he'd be working. After that it was just a question of up, over, out and away.

We'd done the downstairs of the tailor's and we'd gone up to see what more there was. The bodies was in an upstairs room. They'd been killed in a bomb blast a couple of days earlier and no one had discovered them yet. They didn't seem to have any injuries on them. I remember one had his eyes still open. We had a look to see if there was any more gear we could nick and when we was out Dido made a phone call. The good thing was there was no question of the stiffs ID-ing us or giving evidence.

My life changed that night – well it was morning really – in March 1966 when Dicky Hart, who was a Twin hanger-on, tried to shoot me in Mr Smith's Club in Catford and I killed him over it. It was the last time I saw daylight, as it were, for twenty years. Not guilty of murder, five for affray at the Club, ten for the Torture Trial and then another five for leading the Parkhurst Riot. Beatings, solitary, punishment cells, hunger strikes, no home leave, no remission, every letter I received being recorded delivery so they didn't 'get lost'. That was the same with all my sentences.

Whilst I was away the man who give evidence against me in the murder, Henry Botton, got shot himself at his house in Shooters Hill, Greenwich. It was just as well I was away because otherwise I suppose I'd have been the first one to be looked for. I'd served just about seventeen years when he was done in July 1983. He'd been watching a Frank Bruno bout on television when there was a knock on the door, and bang.

It was a bit of a funny killing. Billy Clarkson, from a good South London family, got life for it. He'd given the contract to a kid who'd dressed up like a policeman so's Botton wouldn't sus when he opened the door. It was Botton's own fault, really. He was out grassing again; giving evidence against Billy in a conspiracy case.

After that when I come out in 1987 there was a two stretch over some stolen coins and that was the end of my villainy. Then come the books and what with the radio and telly shows and the advertisements and a couple of films, my life has changed.

I come from a good but poor family. My father was half Red Indian and I think he did a bit of time for manslaughter in Canada as a boy but thieving, never. The same with my mother. She had three jobs to help keep the family going. There are five kids and we're all still alive. Twins, a boy and a girl, and another sister who've never been in trouble in their lives, and Eva and me who have been the villains. Well, Eva's never been a villain. She had a bit of form for hoisting, and her only other trouble came when she got a three over trying to get a witness to tell the truth in the Torture Trial. My eldest three boys have all done some heavy work and taken heavy bird to go with it, but my last played football for Brighton and he's another with never a day in trouble.

When I was growing up the top men in London were the Sabinis from Clerkenwell. They was interned in the war and Alf White from Kings Cross took over. He'd been one of their men in the 20s. After him come Jack Spot and Billy

Hill in the late 40s and more or less straight after come the Twins. Of course, there was all sorts of other families all over London. The ones I had the most trouble with were local to Camberwell, the Carters. They'd been great friends of the Brindles, but by the time Eva married Jimmy Brindle they was quarrelling. That's about all the background you need to know if you haven't read my other books.

I watched that television interview with Reggie earlier this year. The one where he's in bed all tubed up. People made a lot about him having admitted to one more killing, but I notice that he never said who he killed. If he was making a confession then you'd have thought he'd have said it was Mad Teddy Smith, who everyone supposed it was. Got it all off his chest. What was the point of keeping it back? The story was that Ronnie and Teddy had had a row over a boy down at Steeples Bay in Kent, and a few weeks later Teddy had simply disappeared. The SP was that Ronnie and Reggie had done him together, but if that is right then it makes no sense that Ronnie said he'd done his – meaning George Cornell – and Reggie should get on and do his when Jack McVitie was killed in Evering Road. If it was right about Teddy then it meant Reggie had already done his. And as I've said before, I heard it from a good source that Teddy knew what was likely to happen and went to Australia, well out of the way. He wouldn't be the first.

When I went to see Reggie in his hotel up in Norwich just before he died I was thinking how things and places have changed. The Twins are gone and so is their brother, Charlie; Darby Sabini and his brothers; Alf White and his boy Harry; Billy Hill; Jack Spot; Ruby Sparks, the great jewel thief; Dodger Mullins and his mate Timmy Hayes; George and Jimmy Wood, who came from West Ham; the climber 'Taters' Chatham, and so is Billy Benstead. That really good man Billy Howard, who more or less was King of the Elephant in his day and had the Beehive Club in

Brixton, has gone as well. I'm really the only link there is today between old-time villains like the Billies and Ruby and the next few generations.

The streets have gone as well. I walk around London a lot and I look out for places I've known and they just aren't there any more. Bombed and pulled down for rebuilding of railway stations and new office blocks. And if they are still there they're unrecognisable because their names have changed. You try and find Rillington Place where Christie killed the women. The authorities got sensitive and simply changed the name of the street. The place where the acid bath murderer Haigh killed all those people is a Kentucky Fried Chicken. Even bedroom No 4 in the hotel where Neville Heath killed Margery Gardner in the Pembridge Court Hotel in Notting Hill disappeared – the new numbering just skipped her room. If the place isn't pulled down, then it seems when people try to sell somewhere a big crime took place the first time there's a big mark down, but after that there's no difference. I was in the nick with both Heath and Haigh. I saw Heath when he was in the condemned cell but I never spoke to him, but Haigh and me were in the hospital together at Brixton. I'd been put in there whilst I was on trial for the theft of a torch. The reason was I'd only been out of Broadmoor a bit and they wanted to keep an eye on me. As for Haigh, well he killed a number of people and then boiled them down. All for money. He put it about he drank their blood, but the Pros said that was only to try and get an insanity. He was always well-spoken and polite in the nick. You'd think there was nothing wrong with him. But did he drink their blood? I couldn't tell you. If I had to say one way or the other, it would be that he didn't – but you can never tell for sure unless you're there.

Another thing that has gone are the Rowton Houses, those old dosshouses, turned now into smart hotels. There was a very big one down Kings Cross; it's a Holiday Inn now. A fellow who was living in one pulled a twelve year PD and left his clothes and suitcase there. Whilst he was away he wrote a couple of letters but he didn't get a reply, which wasn't surprising when you think of how letters went missing in the nick. After he come out he went back and found the place had got converted and all his stuff had been chucked away. He really went to town. He told me he got quite a bit of compensation for all the suits and a dinner jacket he never had. Good luck to him.

As for names of people, Billy Hill had just about everyone in his book *Boss of Britain's Underworld*, but he mostly had them under different names. I suppose I'm one of the few left who can work most of them out. I'm there but my name is spelled differently. Franney the Spaniel was Franny Daniels; Timber Jim and Wooden George from Ilford were the Wood brothers; good men too. The Whites were the Blacks; Teddy Odd Legs was Teddy Hughes because he had a limp. Big Jock was Jock Wyatt; and Jack Spot was Benny the Kid. Teddy Machin was Terrible Ted. Italian Jock and Italian Albert were Victor and Albert Dimes. Jimmy Emmett was Flash Jimmy. He cut Dodger Mullins and Billy Hill's brother, Archie, in the West End. As a result Billy cut him rotten near the Paramount Dance Hall, which used to be in Tottenham Court Road. Emmett went on to draw a ten. He shot at a man near the Café de Paris in Coventry Street where Princess Margaret used to go, but missed him. I'm not sure she wasn't actually in the place at the time but, whatever, the authorities weren't having people using guns when she might be at risk so an example had to be made. You wouldn't have marked Jimmy as a man who used guns but he had a bad mouth when he'd been drinking.

There's so many things changed, so I thought I'd put down the real names and the places where me and others have been over the years and what we did there before everything is forgotten.

SOUTH LONDON

1

I was born at home, which was a minute from Waterloo Station; fifteen seconds if you hurried. All five of us was. There was the Lying In Hospital just down York Road – it's derelict now – but to get in there in those days cost money which my parents didn't have. To get to our house you came out the Waterloo Road entrance to the station just where Dartmoor Annie and later Buster Edwards from the Train had their flower stalls, down the steps and across the street right into Cornwall Road, and our place was just about opposite Roupell Street. It was still standing until about eight years ago when they knocked it down to make way for the extension to the Jubilee Line. Opposite us on the corner was a newsagent's. Now it's a smart baker's, Konditori & Cook, but on the other corner was a barber's shop and there's still one there. Valentino's it's called now.

If you walked a few yards towards the river, on the same side of the street as us was St Patrick's Church and the school with its green shamrocks on the wall, It's a nursery school now. Opposite was the Cornwall Club, which was a snooker club, and upstairs they'd sometimes have dances. Me and Billy Murray and another boy did it when we was about ten. We got over the roof and come in round the back, but next door was a police hostel named after Edward Henry, who had a lot to do with fingerprinting in its early days and who became a commissioner, I think. There was a copper leaning out the window and he saw us.

Billy and me went off to Olympia and the circus there, where we picked up some more dough saying we'd mind cars. We got to see the circus as well but when we got back to his place the coppers was waiting. The club was very good though, they wouldn't pros us at all. Billy and his family lived about two minutes away in Doon Street opposite where Bowaters, the paper people, used to put their lorries. They had a dock there. The City of London Corporation used to have their dust carts tip the rubbish onto barges to be taken out to the North Sea. Every year they'd give a party for the locals as a sweetener because the smell was something awful. We always used to be told by the dockers and stevedores not to swim near Waterloo Bridge because of the currents, so we swam by the Oxo building.

Another time Billy and me screwed a billiards' hall and took away a set of balls. They were very valuable and we took them to a youth club just opposite the Lying In Hospital, said we'd found them. We were very popular. That was a place chosen to have girls do some dance before Princess Alice at the Albert Hall. My sister Eva was one of the girls. I remember my Mum doing her best to make Eva look smart for that night. Of course they only wore their uniforms. There wasn't any money for anything else.

When I was about five my parents moved a couple of hundred yards away to Howley Place. It has gone now but it's just where the Chez Gerard restaurant is as you go up the steps to the station. That's where I ran out into the road and got knocked down asking drivers for cigarette cards. They put me on the back of a lorry and took me to St Thomas' Hospital; I had a fractured skull and then I got meningitis. Howley Place took a fair beating in the war. We was number 6 and the first five all got bombed. On one side of the road running up to the bridge there was little hotels, not much more than case joints really, and on the other there was shops. There was also a pub, the Feathers, which was really two pubs. One on the corner of Belvedere Road and Commercial Road, and the other up in Waterloo

Road. On the river side of York Road where the Festival Hall site is now there was hotels for commercial travellers.

I tried a bit of hotel creeping as a kid, nothing much just the cheaper hotels around Waterloo, like those in York Road, and sometimes over into the Strand, but it wasn't really my game. If you was stopped it would be either 'Have you got a job?' or 'I'm looking for Uncle Harry and I think he's in room whatever'. Of course, a scruffy little kid like me couldn't expect to have his Uncle Harry staying in the Savoy. I did a couple of jobs later but only when they was put up by a very good source, otherwise it was a dot in the dark. You could come a real tumble hotel creeping if you weren't careful. Just like me and Jimmy Brindle and Jimmy Humphries nearly did in the Howard Hotel over off the Embankment, when we was trying to raise funds for Jack Rosa's appeal. The police tried to let the jury know we'd got form, and if it hadn't been for the juror who knew what was what we'd have been onto a seven.

Walk on down past the Lying In Hospital in York Road and you come to Leake Street. That's where me and Dido Frett, Gerry Newman and Danny Swain had a really good tickle at the end of the war. There was all arches with lock-up warehouses in them with stuff like Scotch inside. They had double doors with padlocks on them almost as it looks now. If the doors was open they'd be well guarded, but by chance when we was having a look round we saw in the first arch on the left that there was Scotch being kept there. It's amazing how there really wasn't any security, not belled up or anything. Just a man who acted as caretaker who lived in a house at the end of the road and kept an eye on things. We were back that night with the Stillsons and we was away. We went back three months later but this time the man seen us and we had to be on our toes. There wasn't any problem; we was in a hooky van.

As a kid, I earned a fortune out of the station. There wasn't that number of porters and there wasn't any parking attendants so it was a question of 'Look after your car, sir?' again. Or 'Carry your bags, sir?' You could do it all day long and some people was in such a hurry they'd give you a white fiver to go and buy cigarettes and papers and things and that's the last they'd see of me. It didn't happen too often but when I got home with it and told my mother I'd found it, she'd be exclaiming what a lucky child I was to her. She was sensible enough not to tell my father. I'm sure he'd have realised what was going on.

Another place I did well at was The Ring at Blackfriars, where there was boxing twice a week. Joe Reeder had a café almost literally right opposite and I'd mind cars there. My uncle was in the army with him in the First World War and Joe would tell me what cars I shouldn't be looking in. Then suddenly all-in wrestling seemed to take over in the mid 1930s. Not that that did me any harm. There was still cars to be minded even though people didn't come from so far away. People was much more gullible in those days. The man and the woman in the street wouldn't believe you if you said it was hooky.

I think it was because there was talk of plans to knock down Howley Place to make more room for Waterloo Station that, before we were kicked out, my parents decided to move to the Walworth Road. The little place where we'd lived in Howley Place backed on to much bigger houses in Tennyson Street. Ours were two up and two down with a privy in the back yard, but these were on four floors with a few rooms on each floor. As kids we'd keep a look out for which houses were standing empty. There was no question of squatters moving in. Instead we'd steam in and strip the place of lead. The new house had an inside toilet but it still didn't have a bathroom. People kept themselves clean, of course, but a bath wasn't so much of a priority as it is now. If you wanted a bath it was down to Manor Place. It didn't matter you was going in straight after someone else. They had an attendant there whose job it was to clean them; but you had to give him a tip if you wanted him to clean the bath for you. Think how recent it is comparatively that hotels, even quite good ones, have put in private baths.

2

Brasses in Waterloo were really the bottom end of the market. They'd fallen a long way even in their world, down from Mayfair to Soho to Kings Cross and then across the river. They were mostly from up North and I don't remember ever seeing a local girl. Half a crown was what they charged for what they call hand-relief nowadays and five shillings for a knee trembler. Remember, they were making their money off the soldiers who were staying in the Union Jack Club and they wouldn't have much money to lash out. What did a Mickey Bolger get a week before the war? A quid? We'd shout at them as kids 'Fucking old brass' and they'd give us sixpence to go away. The brasses lived in them little hotels, well they weren't much better than dosshouses, along the arches by Howley Place. My Gran used to cook and clean in one. The brasses would toss their rubbish out into our street. No wonder there was rats. You couldn't leave your door open in case they run in.

With the brasses about and the disgrace of a decent girl getting knocked up there was always work for the local abortionists. In fact, that was one of those crimes like bigamy which increased in wartime. With people not knowing what was going to happen the next day they took more chances. Of course, abortion was a crime which didn't get reported unless something went wrong. Before the war there was something like 150 prosecutions a year, but by the end of the war there was nearer 650 and God knows what the real abortion figure was.

The abortionist was really a part of the neighbourhood. Everyone knew who they were but people didn't look down on them. Mind you, it could be a risky business. As I say, usually it only came on top if something happened and the girl had to go to hospital or even died, but at the end of the war there was one old woman, Miriam Palmer her name was, come from Penfold Street, Camberwell, who was done at the Bailey. She was a bit unlucky. She'd scraped a girl and so far as I know it had turned out all right. Then the girl suddenly decided she wanted her money back; reckoned it was too much. She went round and said if the old woman didn't give her back the £50 she paid she'd go to the police. Miriam says she's not going to be blackmailed and tells her to go and do just that and that's what she did. The Pros made a big fuss, saying that what was so serious about the case was the high price Miriam was charging. She got three years. She was 69 at the time. That was a hard sentence for a woman then.

The other thing people got away with more was doing wives who'd been unfaithful during the war whilst they was overseas. There was one case, in Fulham it was, when the fellow came home bringing his rifle with him and laid in wait for his wife and her boyfriend and shot her in the bedroom. The jury brought in manslaughter and the judge just gave him fifteen months. Then there was another case down in Poplar where the husband stabbed his wife in the lung. She'd been having it off whilst he was away. The brief, Birkett, who'd defended Bert Marsh and Bert Wilkins over the dog track killing at Wandsworth and was now a judge, was really sympathetic and give him just two days.

One of the brasses from the Waterloo Road copped it in 1942. Peggy Richards' body was found just by Waterloo Bridge. Someone had tried to strangle her and there were bruises all over her body. Then a funny thing happened. A Canadian soldier called McKinstry went to the police and handed in her handbag. Of course, that was just asking to be arrested. He said they'd been together and quarrelled, then she'd hit him with her handbag and run off leaving him holding it. No one in the cops believed him and he got charged with murder. But, when it came to it, no one could say he wasn't telling the truth and I'm glad to say he got chucked.

Well before my time, but a man who definitely murdered some brasses round here was also said to have made a remark, when he was swinging for the murder of Matilda Clover, about his being Jack the Ripper. Though with the hood over his head I don't know how they could have heard. He was Neill Cream, and he lived in the Lambeth Road.

Cream had been born in Scotland in 1850 to a big family who went to Canada when he was a boy. He'd gone to McGill College at Montreal to study medicine and he did well and graduated. That was when he became involved with a Flora Brooks, whose father owned a hotel. Good start for a young man you might think, but he went and put her in the family way, which was a disgrace in them days. Then he applied his medical skills and aborted her. She nearly died as a result. That was when her father found out and Cream was forced to marry. The marriage didn't last long because he walked out the following day, sailed to England and enrolled at St Thomas' Hospital. After that he went up to Edinburgh and got another qualification there.

He then went back to Canada to continue his career as an abortionist, but either he was unlucky or he wasn't very good or he was doing so many that the law of averages caught up with him, because he was nearly nicked after Kate Gardener, a young chambermaid, was found dead in a lavatory near his rooms. Wisely, he moved to Chicago where he opened a surgery on Madison Avenue, and again was fortunate to avoid a conviction when a girl called Julia Faulkener died. By now he was also peddling pills as a remedy for epilepsy.

From the pictures he wasn't what you'd call a good-looking man – for a start he'd got a very nasty squint – but he could certainly pull the women. A railway agent and epileptic Daniel Stott sent his young wife, who was also called Julia, to Cream to collect his pills and it wasn't that long before Stott himself had to go – poisoned. I don't know what Cream was thinking. He'd got away with it until he sent a message to the coroner blaming the pharmacist for supplying the wrong pills. The man wasn't having it and the end result was that Cream got life in Joliet.

Again he had a bit of luck. His father died and left him $16,000 which wasn't a bad sum in them days. He was released for good behaviour in July 1891, went to Canada to collect his dough and sailed for England. At the beginning of October he took up lodgings at 103 Lambeth Palace Road. Two days after settling in he met a young brass, Matilda Clover, and then purchased a quantity of poison. She wasn't his first victim.

On 13 October Ellen Donworth collapsed outside the Wellington Public House in the Waterloo Road. She was taken to hospital but she died before she ever got there. She'd managed to say she had met 'a tall gentleman with cross eyes, a silk hat and bushy whiskers'. He'd been carrying a bottle of white stuff from which he had persuaded her to drink.

Poor Matilda Clover met up with him a week later. She knew him as Fred, took him back to her lodgings at 27 Lambeth Road and died in agony there. This time Cream had a bit more luck with the coroner because her death was put down to *delirium tremens* as a result of alcoholism.

Cream really was on a roll because within the week he picked up a Louise Harvey at the Alhambra Theatre and spent the night with her in a hotel in Berwick Street in the West End. The next evening he met her again and give her some pills to take, but she threw these over the Embankment into the river.

He never seemed to learn from his mistakes because he started writing letters again. One was to a Dr Broadbent who practised in Portman Square, near where Charlie Richardson had a tame doctor in the 1960s, accusing him of doing Matilda and asking for £2,500. He also sent a letter to the Countess Russell, who was staying at the Savoy, accusing her husband of the same thing. I don't know how he picked him out. It's funny but no one seems to have taken any notice.

It wasn't until the next spring that he was at it again. He'd been to Canada and within ten days of getting back he poisoned a pair of young brasses from Brighton who were then lodging at 118 Stamford Street, Waterloo.

He must have really been off his rocker because firstly, he suggested to his landlady that another of the tenants at 103 Lambeth Palace Road, a medical student called Walter Harper, was the murderer of the two girls. She thought he must be mad and so she did nothing. Then Cream wrote to Harper's father claiming that he had proof that his son had murdered the two girls. If, however, Dr Harper cared to send him £1,500 he'd keep stumm. You'd think Harper would have done something but he didn't. He just took no notice and Cream did not persist.

Next, Cream took an acquaintance, John Haynes, on a tour of the murder spots, rather like I do with my tour, and discussed the cases in some detail. He really did want to do for himself because he also talked to another man, McIntyre, who turned out to be a copper. That was it.

He was arrested on 3 June 1892 and told the police 'You have got the wrong man, but fire away'. They dug up the body of Matilda Clover and a jury brought in a verdict that she had been killed by Cream. In them days a jury could name an actual person as the murderer. I think Lord Lucan was the last person named before they decided the law was unfair and changed it. Cream was up at the Old Bailey before the hanging judge Hawkins and was sentenced to death on 20 October. He was topped at Newgate on 15 November which is when he called out 'I'm Jack . . .' which at the time people thought meant he was saying he was Jack the Ripper. Now, people think that he was ejaculating. Some men, like that Tory MP a few years ago, like to strangle themselves when they're flogging themselves and maybe it was a question of his coming as he went, so to speak.

Talking of Stamford Street where the last two girls died, the first man I ever knew who was killed lived there. When I heard I can't say I was sorry. Thomas Meaney his name was. He was one of them Holy Joes you come across. He also thought of himself as a great practical joker. He worked for Scotland Yard driving the Black Maria, although he wasn't a copper himself, and he knew my family. In fact he took me up boxing at Scotland Yard and was very friendly with my family. Then the day I got nicked for stealing cigarettes from a little shop in Stamford Street he was the driver of the van I was put in. You'd think he'd be properly sympathetic or have the decency to say nothing but no. There he was upsetting my mother with his false words of advice. That was in the 30s of course.

Anyway he was a great boozer and when he was living in the flats in Peabody Buildings in December 1950 he went out drinking with an Irish mate, Billy Donoghue. When they got back to Billy's flat, Billy collapsed on the sofa and Meaney got on the bed. When Billy woke up, still half boozed, he saw what he thought was a dummy under the covers left by Meaney and he went and stabbed it.

Then, of course, he discovered his mistake. I'm glad to say they dropped the murder and he only got three years for manslaughter.

3

In some ways Walworth hasn't changed that much since I was a boy. When I was about twelve my parents moved from Waterloo to a flat over some shops just opposite and a bit down from what was the Reform Club. That was where Charlie and Eddie did Jack Rosa after Eva's husband had been given a bashing, and is now the Castle Hotel at the beginning of the Walworth Road. I don't think the move was anything to do with the council. They just moved. There was only Eva and me left at home now. All the others were gone, either married or living with someone.

The place where they moved to went up in the war but the arches where the Elephant Snooker Club was situated still stand. My sister Eva and her mates used to sleep on and under the snooker tables in the bombing. They thought it was safer but it was a daring thing for a young girl to go into a snooker club, let alone sleep in one in them days. I don't know about it being that much safer either. A load of slate coming down on you wouldn't do you much good.

The pub, the Hampton Court Palace, hasn't changed a bit. That's just round the corner in Hamilton Place. It was where my old friend Jimmy Robson saw off Lennie Garrett who'd kicked a pregnant woman. Lennie and his brothers lived just down from the Hampton Court and Jim went round to his home and when Lennie pulled a knife Jim did him with a dustbin lid. Of course there were reprisals.

Before he got married Jim had lived with his parents about quarter of a mile down at No 1 Manor Place. There's a doctor's surgery there now. Once he got married he moved to Brixton. Lennie and some others came round looking for Jim. The night they did him, a bit after eleven, I was in a café, the Cabin, near the big church in Brixton with Dido Frett and Johnny Carter – I was friends with him then. A couple, George and Mary, owned it and they could often get a steak off the market. It was one of the places the chaps went to after the pubs closed. Lennie came in that night, looked round and went out. I didn't think nothing of it, but so far as he was concerned, once he hadn't seen Jim with us in the café then it was odds on where he'd find him.

He went mob-handed to Jim's place and they cut Jim to ribbons and gave his wife Toni a belt for good measure. She was a great friend of Eva – good shoplifter. I went to see Jim in hospital and I put together a little team of people and we sorted them out. December 1944 it was. It took a bit of time to do it but we caught up with them one by one. One of the men with me was Danny Swain, just about the best driver you could ever have. In the war if he was being chased he'd make a turn into a side street, get up on the pavement and wiggle his way between the rubble and the lamp posts. You wouldn't have thought you could get a car down the street but Danny could. He'd got cat's eyes. The coppers would simply continue on down the main road. All they'd see was a concrete block closing off the road. Poor Danny, he had Alzheimer's but I believe he's dead now.

Jim and Lennie finally sorted out their problem down Aggie Hill's club in Soho. Jim was going in there when a fellow said 'You know Lennie and the firm are in there'. That wasn't going to stop Jim but he borrowed a knife off the bloke. Lennie just came over to Jim and said 'Isn't it about time we buried the hatchet?' And Jim agreed. Strangely enough they bumped into each other in the Walworth Road the very next day.

Oddly enough, Jim had always been friends with Lennie, who was known as a good thief himself. He'd been a professional boxer before the war and he'd go out breaking with Jim. You could rely on him. Once, when Jim fell through a roof, Lennie came and picked him up and got him to hospital. A less good man would have scarpered. Lennie also got out of Lambeth Magistrate's Court, which was a small place in Renfrew Road just off the Elephant. It's long been closed now – during the war I think it was. He climbed to the ceiling of the prisoners' waiting room and broke through a skylight and got away through the local hospital grounds. At the end of the war he was back yet again, this time charged with doing a copper. The beak was going to give him bail because he said his wife was pregnant. Then it turned out he wasn't married and the stipe changed his mind.

The last I heard of Lennie was when I read in the papers that he'd been given a right seeing to. It must be five years ago.

Jim's about five years older than me but even so we quickly became friends. He was a good thief and he had a good name to him. He always used to carry a knife with him. In the Blitz when the windows of a shop or office went in there'd be cardboard put up and Jim used to cut holes in it so he could hand the stuff out. In those days we'd wear a tin helmet and an arm band so if anyone saw us they'd think we were the ARP. There was a lot of looting by people in the ARP, let alone us.

Jim got a four in February 1946 with Jerry Callaghan, from the big South London family, who got a 21 months, and then Jim pulled a long stretch in July 1960 when he was done on two separate jelly cases. He got a ten on the first and the judge gave him fourteen consecutive. We had a benefit for Jim just recently, on 2 July, at the Masons Arms pub in East Street, Walworth. It was his 84th birthday – and it was very good. Johnny Foy was with him.

He was doing life and the judge tried to make his sentence for the jelly consecutive and all. Johnny Foy had been given life for robbery in Manchester in 1959. There was some talk he'd thrown corrosive fluid in the victim's face, which is why he'd got such a long stretch. Two years into his sentence in January 1961 they were transferring him from Strangeways to Dartmoor when he jumped off a moving train. They didn't pick him up again until the July, when they surrounded the place he was staying in Lord Street in Blackpool.

Johnny was lucky, throwing himself off the train like that. Just about the end of the war another fellow called Fernie, a smash and grab man, wasn't at all. You used to be taken to the Moor by special train from Waterloo once a month. The vans would come onto the platform and you'd be handcuffed, sometimes on a chain, and loaded on the train. Once you were in the carriages things was a bit relaxed and your relatives could come and bring you food, which you could have with you provided it was all eaten by the time you got to the Moor. Anyway Fernie had always sworn he wasn't going back to Dartmoor, and on his way to the lavatory he broke out of his cuffs and got onto the running board of the compartment. Quite a lot of people tried to escape from that train, and usually the screws would pull the communication cord and that was when a man would take his chance and jump as the train slowed, but it didn't happen on this occasion. Fernie jumped and was killed when he landed on his head.

They stopped taking them to Dartmoor by train whilst I was away in the 60s. You could save your visits if you was on the Moor and have them all in your local nick over a couple of weeks. So when Jimmy Andrews from Islington come up and finished his visits whilst he was doing a seven I knew he'd be going back, and I went along to Pentonville to make sure he got his parcel of food. I met a half hooky screw outside and asked when Jimmy would be going to the station and he said, 'He's gone, Frank. They do it by coach now'. I hadn't heard.

It's funny, throwing vitriol was very big up until the war but it died out after that. Eddie Guerin, who got off Devil's Island in the early years of the last century, made a speciality of that. In the early 30s friend Tommy Speedles got ten years for slinging vitriol in the face of a West End brass, Fanny Simmonds, who was known as Polish Fanny, at Wimbledon dog track. She was in a terrible state. They'd been together for years and they'd been high on the hog when he was winning on the dogs, and when he wasn't then he'd had her on the game. As often as not pimps did it a lot to their brasses. I should think that Tommy Speedles was the last I heard of.[1]

But, getting back to Jimmy Robson, he got made a trusty red band whilst he was in Parkhurst, after working in the laundry. It was through him the football team, the Soho Rangers, with me and a load of others, played the prisoners on the island. Jim did lots of good work whilst he was a trusty. He'd got a screw squared and Jim's wife, Toni, and a man would come down to the island and give the screw quite a bit of dough – maybe even up to two grand. It would be marked down to various men: fifty to this one, a hundred to that. The screw would act as a sort of banker so a man could say he'd like two ounces of tobacco that week or five if he was treating someone and the screw would get it for him. It was much better than the man having a whole load in his cell at one time and maybe getting caught and not being able to explain it. Of course there was some risk for the screw and he took half the money. Being that Jim was a trusty working in the laundry

---

[1] For an account of Tommy Speedles and his part in the Dartmoor Mutiny of 1931 see *Mad Frank and Friends*, Chapter 1.

he could get round the prison more or less as he liked, seeing people and taking their orders for tobacco.

It wasn't that difficult to have a screw straightened. I had one in Birmingham once. Eva would send registered letters with the money to a con who'd been discharged and the con would deal with the screw. Then the con got nicked and put up the screw's name. Eva got interviewed and said it was ridiculous and a solicitor came down to see me on the Moor where I'd been transferred. It all blew over and as far as I know the screw went on to be a principal officer.

Jim eventually got out in the early 70s through Billy Hill and his friend, Percy Horne, who'd been in Borstal with Bill before the war and was doing good in the contracting business. Bill suggested that Jim write from prison asking Percy for a job. Percy wrote back to the Governor saying he'd like to help but he normally liked to see a man before he took him on. Of course it was just to give Jim a visit because he was always going to take Billy's recommendation. Percy had a contract to pull down Nine Elms at the time before they built the flower market there. All Jim had to do was make the tea (Dido worked there with him, Percy was very good there) and take the copper to the scrap merchant once a week. Percy was clever there. He'd share out the money from the copper with his boys. As soon as all the metal was gone they'd be off to another job. Percy was also a brilliant pianist and there was nothing he liked better of a Friday evening than to have a sing-song in the pub. The landlords loved him. Free entertainment.

I did a pub at the end of Browning Street where I live now on behalf of the landlord of the King's Arms. Cis and Vic Rosati owned it. He'd been the potman in Cis's father's place, the Duke of Clarence at St George's Circus in the London Road. Before that Vic was about a bit with the Sabinis. They took the Kings Arms in 1937 or the year after. It was almost opposite the old Reform Club. It was the place to go of an evening if you were looking for someone because there weren't telephones then, let alone mobiles like there are today. You might go to one or two other places, but the chaps would all end up in the King's Arms before closing time.

Anyway, Vic and Cis were sort of pioneers. They'd have singers and maybe a small band in; they didn't have to pay them, just pass the hat around. Well, the landlord of this pub in Browning Street started doing the same thing and it wasn't good for Vic's trade. The man wouldn't be told so I went round and did his place up – all the windows – and he soon got the message. I think Vic give me £30 for my trouble, which wasn't bad dough. And then if I was ever in with him and I was a bit skint I'd look at him, pat me waistcoat pockets and he'd give a nod saying it was all right, I didn't have to pay, it was on the house. The pub I did is an Irish pub today – The Stroke of Luck. I can't for the life of me think what it was called back then.

During the war at the end of an evening you'd go to someone's house and have a party. Charlie Saye was one of those people who made a bit of money letting people use his flat. His daughter, Gladys, was another of Eva's pals. There was early closing in the war and anyway there wasn't all that much booze in the pubs. So what people did was have chaps round their house at ten bob a head. The punters had to bring their own booze, beer and Scotch they'd nicked off a lorry. If you'd had a lorry of spirits you were in for a nice few quid. Letting people in for these parties was a precarious living because there was always the chance that a fight would break out and all the furniture would get smashed. These parties went on after the war and some time in the 1950s Charlie had a little mob in his place one night and the place got smashed up and him and his wife took a few digs. I'm not sure he didn't nick them over it.

Outside the Duke of Clarence was where some of the Carter family did Hoppy Smith in 1942. Hoppy's sister was once married to 'Tom Thumb' Brindle of the family my sister, Eva, married into. Tom's second wife was the daughter of a policeman, but that was when he was becoming respectable. Hoppy was a big man, well over six foot and with a club foot which is how he got his name. He was a sort of thieves' ponce and a bit of a con man as well. One of his tricks came if you'd done a job. He'd say he could place the tom for you but he never really tried and then you'd have to pay him for his time. It was his way of taking a few quid off of you.

Hoppy was a beast with a razor and he didn't half cut some people in his time. He cut Harry Carter in another pub, the Flowers of the Forest, and cut Johnny Carter's tie off at the same time. They met up with him a week later in the Duke of Clarence, called him out and were giving it to him when he picked up a child out of its pram. At that time people could leave a child out on the street whilst they went and had a drink and it was perfectly safe, no question of anyone stealing it. Anyway Hoppy picks up the kid and holds it as protection and, of course, with that the Carters backed off. They weren't going to hurt a child.

4

One of the local heroes I was told about in my childhood was Gerald Chapman whose mother had been a washer-woman in Camberwell, I never knew quite where. Chapman was big time in America where he was also known as Lord Reginald Francis and Major Leslie Chapman as well as the Monocled Bandit. I must have been four when they topped him, but he was still talked about in my youth.

It's as they say, prison is a breeding ground for crime. That's where you learn your trade. Chapman started off being put in what they called a House of Refuge when he was a kid, and then took up doing burglaries and went on to a reformatory, and then he got three years in Sing Sing. Then when he came out of that he quickly got twelve for trying to shoot a copper who was after him for a domestic burglary. By the time he got out from that one it was the Prohibition era and he teamed up with George 'Dutch' Anderson who he'd met in the nick and who really taught him the trade.

They got over two million dollars in a mail robbery in 1921 and another $70,000 about six weeks later. Then someone shopped him and he got 25 years. He was sent to the penitentiary in Atlanta and in 1923 he escaped and was in a gun battle with the cops about 70 miles away. They captured him and took him back to the nick, and he got out of the hospital with a bullet in his arm and two in his kidney.

Then Dutch Anderson escaped as well. Both of them came back to England and Scotland Yard tried searching around Camberwell but they could not find them. From the stories, Chapman returned to America and lived in New York where he was known as the Count of Gramercy Square. Then in October 1924 he was found blowing a safe and he shot a police officer dead. By then he was living in Muncie in Connecticut with a farmer and his wife. He was spotted, and I don't know how it come about, the people gave evidence against him – probably to save themselves from getting nicked for harbouring him. As a result they were shot dead on his behalf by a man nicknamed One-Armed Wolfe, who got life for his trouble.

Anyway Chapman's execution was fixed for 28 February 1926 but he said he could not be hanged until he had completed 20 out of his 25 year sentence – the one he'd escaped from – a question of life and death consecutively. So Coolidge, who was the President, pardoned him and Chapman went and rejected the pardon. If he hadn't they'd have topped him straight away. Then there was a long legal battle as to whether a man could refuse a pardon, but of course they weren't going to give him the chance of another escape and he got topped in April 1926. Dutch Anderson had already gone down when he shot a copper who managed to get the gun and turn it on Anderson. There was a story that Anderson was the son of a high class Danish family and his real name was Ivan Dahl Von Teller, but that sounds like a German name to me.[2]

5

A man who went down in 1945 was Frank Everitt, known as Duke, a taxi driver. He was found in Lambeth Bridge Pumphouse on Lambeth Bridge Road in the early hours of 18 October. He'd been shot behind the left ear and it was reckoned the shooting had been done in his cab. They found his taxi over in Notting Hill Gate. Everitt was one of those people who led a double life because, after the initial comments about how could anyone do this to such a lovely man, it turned out he was also in the black market. He'd been a copper himself and then he'd turned private detective. For an ex-copper he'd managed to pick up a lot of property, because he had a place in Soho and another in Ealing and he'd just bought a bungalow in Gloucestershire. One of Scotland Yard's so called Big Eight, Walter Chapman, was in charge. When there was an inquest the next year Chapman said they was still looking but there was never any arrests made. In fact when those two Poles, Grondkowski and Malinowski, was in the condemned cell over the killing of Russian Robert, the coppers visited them to see if they would admit to doing Everitt as well but they remained staunch. Maybe they hadn't, because one of them might have worked his ticket and got a reprieve if he'd given the other up.

* * *

---

[2] See Chapter 8.

There was a lot of trouble around the Elephant at that time. There was stories that the Boys were banding together again, particularly when Joseph Hussey's body was found in the Thames around the same time. He was partly crippled and he'd been a theatre queue busker. No one was ever done for his murder to my knowledge.

Just before the war the Elephant Boys had been on the rampage and a local shopkeeper, Mark Selby who ran the State Milk Bar in the Walworth Road, committed suicide over them. There's not much doubt someone had been leaning on him; Billy Howard, I wouldn't be surprised. He was the real Governor. Milk Bars was all the rage from America at the time and for a bit after the war. They was all chrome and brightness. There was another one down at the Bricklayers, I recall.

Billy Howard was a big, big man and tough as nails. During the war he was having a real set-to with Spindles Jackson when a bomb went off in Munton Road in 1941. It had landed the year before and no one noticed. They stopped the fight at once and ran to help out. I don't think they ever started it again. Billy had the Beehive Club, a very good little drinker in Brixton just by the railway bridge, and he also had a spieler in Wyndham Road off the Camberwell Road. Tony Mella, Billy Blythe and me was in there when we got a call from Tommy Falco that the Jack Spot-Albert Dimes fight had gone down.

Another man who'd been in America and who you'd see round the Elephant was a fellow who'd had his face covered in tattoos in the days when it wasn't fashionable. He'd been in Chicago and he used to say he'd been Al Capone's chauffeur. Then he came back here and got done for stabbing a man in Ruislip. Seven years he got. His name was Jacobus Van Dyn. His was a funny case. Within a few months of getting his bird he was released just like that, but he could never get the pardon he wanted. He was still trying 30 years later, saying if they'd just re-open the case he could prove his innocence. In the meantime he'd joined a circus and toured as a sort of freak 'The Worst Man in the World'. He lived in Parkview House, now a hotel, just by the Elephant. If he was alive now he could go to that new Criminal Review Commission, but he'd have to be at least a hundred.

I don't like tattoos myself and I've never had one. My Dad had a couple of small ones but that was natural, his having been in the Navy, but it's not for me.

6

I do a lot of walking about the place and the other day I was down in Wyndham Road in Camberwell where Charlie Richardson's mother had her shop. It was a sort of general grocery store. She was well loved. If people was skint she'd always give them tick. Eva and her husband, Jim, lived just round the corner.

There was a good murder there years ago. Edgar Edwards attacked and killed John William Darby and his wife, Beatrice, on 1 December 1902. They had a small but profitable grocery shop at number 22 when Edwards arrived carrying a five-pound sash-weight wrapped in newspaper.

By the time Edwards had left the shop he had nailed up the premises and attached a note saying the business had closed down but would soon re-open under new management. Over the next week, he gave a few shillings to the locals and got them to help empty the contents of the shop and the living quarters, taking them to his new home at 89 Church Road, Leyton. Amongst the contents were black sacks containing the bodies of the Darbys and their young daughter, Ethel, whom he'd strangled and cut up.

When it came to it he was a bit unlucky. The police were called but it wasn't to investigate any murder. It was thought that the Darbys had run off with the Christmas Loan Club savings, amounting to near £200.

For some weeks it looked as though Edwards was going to get away with it but then, with money running out, what he did was go and attack another grocer. This one survived and give the coppers a description. Once they went round to Edwards' home the police found billheads belonging to the Darbys. After that it was into the garden with the spades until they found them.

When he got to the Old Bailey Edwards ran a defence of insanity. He must have been really loopy because his mother and a great-aunt had died insane, his father was an alcoholic, two cousins were mental defectives and there was another in an asylum. He was a bit unlucky but I suppose the jury thought it was just as well to have him out of the way. If you look at the old newspapers he doesn't seem to have minded all that. When the judge put on the black cap Edwards said, 'This is quite like being on the stage'. On his way to the topping shed in Wandsworth he told the prison chaplain 'I've been looking forward to this a lot'. Of course, you can never tell if he was just play-acting.

One thing you saw when I was a boy and you don't any more is people performing in the streets. There used to be a little band, the Luna Brothers, who would come round regularly the same day every week and play. One of them had a sort of piano he put up and there was a trumpet and violin. People would throw coins to them. Then there were others with performing animals. There used to be organ grinders who always had monkeys and I remember a man with a dancing bear, but Animal Rights has put a stop to all that and it's probably just as well.

There was a man called Weatherly with a performing seal who got involved in a murder case our way in West Square just off St George's Road years ago. He'd cart it around with him and it would honk and flap its flippers. He and his missus, Mary, lived in Coraline Buildings in the Square, and she went and fell for a labourer, William Heeley, and went off to live with him. She probably got sick of the smell of the seal. Then she goes and meets her old man in the street and they're back together. It all ended in tragedy because Heeley waited until Weatherly and the seal were out on the streets doing their act and then he went round to Coraline Buildings and cut Mary's throat. Next he barricaded himself in the flat and cut his own. Poor Weatherly was so upset he tried to drown himself in the seal's barrel, but luckily for one of them he made a mess of it and lived.

The war was a good time to commit a murder. With the Blitz and all the bombs falling and so much rubble about it was easy for someone to go missing and no one thought too much about it. The husband or wife could always say they'd gone to relatives in the country or that they went missing in the Blitz. That's what happened with Harry Dobkin and his wife Rachel, whom he buried in the crypt in the Baptist Church in St Oswald's Place off Kennington Lane.

It was a big trial and that Mr Justice Lawton, whose father I hanged all those years ago when he was governor at Wandsworth, and who give me ten years and poor Charlie 25 at the end of the Richardson Trial, always used to say that was how he got his chance as a barrister.

Dobkin and his wife didn't get on at all. Theirs had been one of those Jewish arranged marriages back in 1920 and they'd had a kid but they'd split up within three years. She went to the local Magistrates' Court and got a maintenance order but it didn't do her much good. He didn't want to pay and if you don't want to there's plenty of ways you can string an order like that out. She had him put away a few times for non-payment and when he was out and they met he'd give her a clip now and again. So then she took out assault summonses on four occasions. That didn't do her much good either because the beaks threw them out.

Then they went and met over in a café in Dalston for tea on Good Friday 1941 and after they left there in the early evening she was never seen again. The next day her sister reported her missing, blaming Dobkin, but like I say there was plenty of missing people then. In fact he took her handbag to Guildford and left it there on a post office counter to make it look like she'd been in Surrey. When it was opened they found a card of a spiritualist and when the woman was contacted she said that Rachel had been hit over the head and done in.

So then the police got round to having a word with Harry Dobkin a few days later – 16 April it was, the day after a small fire broke out in the cellar of the Baptist Church where he was a firewatcher. That same day 23 people were killed when a landmine was dropped 250 yards from the church. It had already been blitzed in August 1940. The police circulated a description of the missing Rachel Dobkin but no one ever said they'd seen her, which wasn't really surprising.

It wasn't until two years later when they were pulling down the church for safety that they found her body, and when they did a post-mortem it turned out she'd been strangled. When the wife turns up dead, look first at the husband is the golden rule and Dobkin was arrested. At the trial Lawton concentrated on her height. The body was a bit over five foot but he got in evidence that she'd been a couple of inches taller and so it couldn't be her body. There was no question of DNA back then, of course, and since she'd never been arrested there were no fingerprints to compare. Eventually her sister, who said she was the same height, was measured and they found that, in her shoes, she was 5′ 1″. That did for Harry. The jury took only twenty minutes to find him guilty. I've often wondered how he persuaded her to come south of the river with him.

7

Tony Reuter was the so-called King of the Teddy Boys who got religion. He was a great cobbles fighter and he took on some of the best. He was with a gang from the Elephant and one of the stories is of a big fight they all had in the Locarno, Streatham. Joey Dunn was the leader of the Brixton boys and Eddie Richardson and Tony and Peter Reuter – with a bit of help – stood up to him and his team.

Peter also faced up to Bobby Ramsey in the Lyceum dance hall off the Strand. Ramsey had once worked with Billy Hill but then got work as a bouncer in that dance hall. I don't know what it was about but Ramsey swallowed it. Peter Reuter took on Eddie Richardson once in the Imperial Billiard Hall at the Elephant and they just about did for each other. They were both standing at the end but they weren't throwing punches. You could fight someone one week and be friends the next day.

Then Billy Graham the Evangelist come over and held all those revival meetings at Earls Court. The idea was that at the end anyone who'd given his life up to Jesus should come forward and the newspapers give Tony Reuter a few quid to join the line. It was all in the papers the next day – what a wonderful convert for the Rev.

Tony was in and out of trouble in the 50s and early 60s. One time he threw a thunderflash at a copper and got five years. Then in 1962 he got off an attempted murder charge. He'd knocked down a Sheila Fraser, no relation. She'd come over the river to a party at a club in Huntley Road, Kennington, with some friends and as she was leaving she remembered she'd left her handbag. She went back and checked to see her dough was still there and people got the hump. Someone threw a glass at her and outside a ruckus started and the coppers said Tony drove the car at her. She was really badly injured and he got a ten. He still lives round the Elephant and I see him quite often. In fact he was round the other day with a copy of Marilyn's *Gangster's Moll* book for her to sign for him.

8

It was in Bagshot Street, Walworth, that Ahmet Abdullah, the fellow known as Turkish Abbi, got shot in March 1991. He was closely related to the Arif family. He was a drug dealer and he'd quarrelled with some other of the South East interests. Abbi got done in the William Hill betting shop. He knew it was on top because he was pleading with his attackers not to kill him. He was shot but he managed to grab one of the other punters as a shield and he got out of the shop before he was shot again. Two brothers, Tony and Patrick Brindle, were done for his murder. It was a funny case. Witnesses were allowed to give evidence from behind screens and they only had to give numbers not their names, and one couple never turned up at all. One went and topped himself. What the Pros maintained was that Abbi had made something like a dying declaration, saying the Brindles had done him.

Tony Brindle said he never knew Abbi from Adam, and when it went down he'd been playing cards and drinking in the Bell in East Street, Walworth. Patrick didn't give evidence. They got chucked in May 1992. Because of the name it was thought that they were related to me through my sister Eva's husband, but they're not. There must be hundreds if not thousands of Brindles over South London. I suppose we may be related but it's fourth cousins twice removed, that sort of thing, if we are. I'm not sure I've ever met them.

Things didn't end there, though. A third brother, David, was killed whilst drinking one evening in the Bell and the man who was just standing next to him got killed as well. Then in 1995 another brother, George, survived being shot from a passing van earlier in the year. No one was nicked for that.

Then in September 1995 Tony was ambushed and shot in Rotherhithe. The story the Pros told the court was that it had been a hit set up by a George Mitchell, a drug dealer in Dublin who is known as The Penguin, on behalf of Peter Daly who'd been financing him. Anyway Michael Boyle got three life sentences for attempted murder and a fellow, David Roads who'd been keeping the guns for him, picked up ten years.

There was some talk Tony Brindle was going to sue the police, because he said they hadn't stepped in quick enough and he'd been hit in the arm, elbow, chest and another couple of places as well. I don't know that anything came of it; I hope something did.

In April this year David Roads got done in an alleyway off Cowper Road in Kingston. He was in Latchmere near Richmond, finishing off his sentence by going out on day release, and he must have been followed on his way back as he tried to get there before the ten o'clock curfew. Shot twice in the head, he was.

9

Brixton was considered quite posh before the war. The ambition of every thief from the Elephant who made it was to buy a house in Brixton. And that lasted up until the 1950s. By then it was falling away but we thought it was posh and Streatham, now that was really posh. Gleneldon Road, Streatham, was where the kid, Tony Baldassare, topped himself. He'd been on the run since he failed to show at the Bailey on a blagging and was surrounded by coppers. He did a magnificent thing. Before he did himself he set fire to all the money he'd nicked so it was never recovered. He used to collect cigarette lighters and he had one in the shape of a coffin. It had his name and date of birth on one side and just 'Died –' on the other. 25 January 1985 it would have been.

Somewhere like Charlton we thought out in the sticks. After all, how many people had cars? Silvertown was just poor. You never went stealing down there; there wasn't nothing to steal. Now with the building going on along the river it might be worth a look.

How things have changed. I remember that police said that one specific day in December 1996 was only the third day there hadn't been a robbery in Brixton in five years. And that was only because they'd been running a big undercover operation.

Charlie Gibbs, he was a good thief. You could touch him for a loan. He was one of them that come from the Elephant and moved to Brixton. I did quite a few jobs with him. The last time I saw him was coming down from Bedford, when we'd been sussed for the snout factory and I got caught. Him and Teddy Gibbs, his brother, were in the car behind and when they could see they couldn't do me no good they peeled off. Then shortly after I went away Charlie got an eight or a ten PD, and whilst he was in the nick he got cancer. It was about that time they brought out the regulation that if you was dying you could be released so you didn't die in the nick. Charlie was one of the very first, if not the first, who was let out. Eva went to his funeral. Charlie's sister, Carrie, was the first wife of Alfie Hinds.

If you went from the Elephant up the New Kent Road and turned into the Old Kent Road then you'd come to an area known as the Bricklayers Arms, which included Bermondsey. It was an old railway depot. People from South London simply called it the Brick, sometimes the Bricklayers. Our world seemed to stop there. It stopped there for a few coppers in the British Transport police back in 1980, when one of them got seven years and another six. They'd been nicking stuff most weekends for eighteen months and they'd got away with something like £364,000 of stuff. Now, even if you know they didn't get the full whack when they knocked it out, it was still good money.

It's always a pleasure to see coppers get done and even better when they turn on each other and start grassing each other to try and get out of things. It doesn't happen often enough, but it did a bit after the war in Catford. In 1949 two young coppers and their sergeant got done for theft and receiving. Mean thing it was too. An old lady had died in Honley Road and the police were called in to look after the house. They didn't guard it all that well because stuff from it turned up in the sergeant's home. There had also been complaints that things had been going off market stalls and a special watch was being kept. The young constable got nicked, and when it all went to the Bailey he said how the sergeant had taken stuff whilst they were inspecting the house and had told him to take something for himself. The second constable had been the one nicking things from the market. One was a load of cami-knickers, which were well fancied then. The copper who give evidence got three years and the one who didn't picked up five. The sergeant copped for a seven.

I used to do a bit of thieving down the railway yards mostly during the war and, often enough, Dave Morbin was with me. In fact he put the idea up. We used to climb onto the skylight, down a rope ladder we brought with us, and we'd have things out of the depot. You wouldn't believe the lax security. Of course, it was blackout and so there weren't lights by which we could be seen, which helped no end. We wasn't the only ones, of course, and someone else come a tumble and that was the end of it. Dave married Lennie Garrett's sister. He died a few years back.

A man who had a club down there was Toby Noble. I think he'd been in the ring at one time. He was a hard-working man but he'd always buy a bit of gear off you. Then he opened a gym and George Daley's brother Tommy ran it for him. You could still see Tommy around at the fights until just a few years ago. A corner man, he was, and a good trainer in his day, but by the end he wasn't doing much more than carry the bucket and sponge.

10

I've never understood why people think it's a good idea to cut bodies in half and then just dump them in the river. They're asking for them to be found. The top half of another body washed up in the river at Battersea just last year. This time it was a young girl, Zoe Parker, who sometimes called herself Cathy Dennis, chopped in half. At first they thought she'd been hit by the propeller of a boat but no, someone had taken a saw to her. It seems she was on the fringes of things, a bit of brassing just to get some money to live. It's no way to make a living at that end of the market, particularly nowadays. There was some research recently which showed that 60 per cent of brasses had been seriously assaulted over the previous months, and another survey showed that a brass is murdered every three to four weeks in Britain. The last I read they hadn't caught anybody, but there was a halfway decent reward on offer.

There was a funny case in Battersea a few years back, around May 1961. One afternoon a doctor's daughter in Chelsea got a call from a man who said his wife was a patient and was ill, could the doctor come? Later they thought the man might have had a Turkish accent or maybe it was a disguise. Anyway, late that night a man comes back to Albert Studios, which was a sort of artists' colony at the back of Albert Mansions in the Albert Bridge

Road, where he lived and found the doctor stabbed to death. The doctor was in his seventies then, Raymond Castillo he was. They could never prove who did it, but the story was that it was another doctor who'd had some sort of quarrel with him.

There was another really funny case in Battersea years ago, well before my time and again it was never solved. You'd hear about these cases in the nick. The screws would talk to an old lag and he'd have told them what really happened and it would get passed on down the line. The screws may even have been in the death cell with someone who'd opened up before he was topped. Remember, there was no wireless, no television and no newspapers for prisoners. We lived on stories about past cons we told each other – nowadays they'd call it oral history.

The man who got killed was a small-time actor, Thomas Weldon Atherston, who appeared in those melodramas that were very popular at the time. In fact he'd been in one, *Grip of the Law*, a couple of weeks before his death. He was found at the back of a house, in Clifton Gardens in Prince of Wales Drive, where his former mistress, Elizabeth Earl, was having supper with Atherston's son Thomas who, just to confuse things, called himself Anderson. A chauffeur heard a couple of shots, saw someone getting over a wall and drove to the police station. When they got back, there was Atherston shot in the face. He had what they called a life-preserver in his hand. A life-preserver could be almost anything provided it was heavy, and you carried it on a loop round your wrist so people couldn't take it away from you and do you with your own weapon. Like coppers and truncheons. The other funny thing was he had his carpet slippers on when he lived miles away.

Elizabeth Earl'd been on the boards herself and was now teaching what they called dramatic art, still do probably. Young Tommy wasn't all that forthcoming, but eventually he said he'd seen his dad die. It was all wonderful for the papers, of course. What was he doing at night with a life-preserver outside his former girlfriend's flat? Everyone had a different theory including one that Elizabeth Earl, Tommy and a younger brother had all conspired to have Dad knocked off. Then there was a theory that he'd come to believe she was having it off with his son and was going to do him, or that there was another lover. The public was well on the side of Miss Earl, and when it came down to it the best theory was that poor old Thomas was simply in the wrong place at the time. He'd gone to see if there was any hanky panky going on but he was shot by a burglar.

People always said that Clapham was pretty free from crime and it certainly was a step up from the Elephant. Mind you, they had a good couple of crimes. In 1953 Michael Davies was done for murder during a gang fight on the Common and it was never really clear he was guilty. Before that I suppose the last really big one was Leon Beron, who was done on the Common on New Year's Eve 1911. Stinie Morrison got sent down for it, but that's a case which has always smelled. No one was ever too clear whether it was just a robbery or whether Leon Beron was a copper's nark, or even if it was something to do with Russian spies. Part of Stinie's trouble was he called a bent alibi and it got shown up. The judge said that foreigners weren't like us and if they told a lie it didn't mean they was guilty, but the jury still put him down. He was reprieved but he did his time the hard way and he died in Parkhurst on hunger strike. He'd had a quarrel with another prisoner and thrown a kitten into a furnace in temper. As a result he'd been given punishment and thought he was being hard done by so he put himself on hunger strike. Of course even that was well before my time, but plenty of people I met in prison had known him in the nick and he was one of the legends.

11

Tony Ash went down in November 1987 when the police shot him at a garage in Sunbury Street, Clapham. I knew him, of course. He was a bouncer at the Frog and Nightgown in the Old Kent Road. He'd once let Charlie Richardson stay at a place he'd had on the coast after Charlie had walked out of the open prison. It was another ready-eye. Tony and Ronnie Easterbrook had give a man £200 to clean and hide a nicked BMW in his garage, but the police give him £1,000 to grass – so there's no prizes which he chose. The job was at a Bejam supermarket in Hare Street, Woolwich. Tony Ash was shot as they went to change cars. Ronnie was shot and all, and got fifteen years as well. He sent a lovely card to the funeral whilst he was on remand 'With sorrow and regard. May your executors and (and he named the man) live long and suffer every day.' What a lovely gesture. There was also a picture of the man on the grave so people could recognise him. It was said there was £35,000 on his head. He got resettled and left his wife to cope with what he'd done. I'm not sure but people say that the whole thing was filmed by Thames Television, since they'd been doing a programme on the squad at the time. Funnily enough, Tony had been involved in the death of two coppers years earlier, when his lorry had jackknifed down in Whitstable and crushed the officers who were in an unmarked car.

There was a whole spate of killings in South London in 1991. That was the year I got shot outside Turnmills in the August. Of course there was the killing of Turkish Abbi in the March, but then there was David Norris who was reckoned to be a supergrass. He was killed at his home in Belvedere in the April. After David Brindle was shot dead in August at the Bell, his friend Perry Donegan was badly injured when he was shot in the leg at the Green Man in the Old Kent Road in November. Meanwhile a fellow called William Walker was shot in the arm and leg when he was walking in Rotherhithe. Then in the early December Kenneth Neal was shot as he left for work with British Telecom from his home off the Old Kent Road. People said that was a mistaken identity. I don't think anyone was ever convicted of any of them.

Another mistaken identity looks like being that of Michael McCormack, who was a director of an indexing firm, and his works manager John Ogden, who were shot on 21 October 1994 in Cavendish Road, Balham. If you looked at it you'd say it was a stone cold contract killing. The fellow who did it was waiting in a sandwich bar and followed the men after they'd had a lunchtime drink in the Prince of Wales public house. He shot them both in the back of the head with a .45 Colt and then ran to a D-registration Vauxhall Cavalier and got clean away. It was later found burned out in Streatham. The coppers discovered it had been bought in a false name for £1,500 cash from some people in Catford, but that was about as near as they ever got. There was talk that whoever did the killing got the wrong pair. Then the next year the coppers had a man on an ID parade. There was talk he'd been in an Open Prison, left for the day, done the shooting and walked back in. Good alibi. He wasn't picked out. Curiously there was another killing in Waterloo a bit before, another drive-by shooting. That car was bought through a newspaper ad and then burned out as well.

Perry Hill, Catford, was where that Andy Birjukove was shot back in September 1993 in the Two Brewers, where he was drinking with his mate Bobby Campbell, the St Mirren footballer. Campbell had once run the Rutland Arms nearby and he got shot as well but he survived. I don't think the locals were too sympathetic about Birjukove. There was stories he'd been dealing in cocaine and ignored people when he was told not to.

12

I suppose one of the oldest cons ever must have been John Day, who was 86 the year I was born. He got fifteen months in the March. He'd been a big burglar in his day and he'd been known as Daylight John because he didn't like working at night, maybe because of the extra bird that would be handed out. He never took any tools with him either; just shoved his shoulder against the door. His speciality was chatting up the housemaid and getting a lie of the land that way, although by the time he last got nicked he was a bit old for that.

This time he just sees a woman leave her house in Ommanney Road, New Cross, and goes and does the front door. He was half away with the jewellery when she comes back because she's forgotten her purse. She grabs hold of him and hollers and some people come to help her. The judge said John was lucky, and if it hadn't been for his age he'd have got longer. He still added in hard labour though and said John was well fit enough for it.

SOHO

1

The first time I went to Soho was when I was a kid. My sister Eva and me and Timmy, our Airedale dog, would go to the baker's just by Gerrard Street to pick up yesterday's bread. If they'd run out we had to walk on through Soho to their other branch the opposite side of Oxford Street. From then on I've been in and out of the West End whenever I've been out of the nick. It's changed over the years, of course. There was no Chinatown like there is today. The old 24-hour Boots in Piccadilly Circus where the druggies used to queue to get their scripts filled after midnight has gone, but the one tucked away on the other side of the Circus, near the Regent Palace Hotel, which was just a small shop when I was a delivery boy for it, has grown and grown. It's huge now.

The hotel's smarter than it was a few years back. When I was young it was always known as an upmarket brasses' hotel or somewhere a woman went without her husband. It went very downmarket. I remember reading of a fellow who was accused of raping a girl on the carpet of the women's lavatory whilst people stood around watching. Her bloke had gone to register and when he came back he found her having it away on the floor. I'll never forget the verbals. This was the Pros's version. The fellow says, 'Hey what are you doing? She's my chick', and the man, who's a soldier in uniform, flicks out his boot at him and says, 'Eff off, can't you see I'm busy?' He got a not guilty, of course, and quite right.

Right on the corner of Shaftesbury Avenue was a newsreel cinema. They were big after the war when there was no television. You didn't pay as much as for a proper cinema and there was the news and a few cartoons and possibly a travelogue. The whole show lasted an hour. They were very popular after something like the Grand National or a big fight because that was the only way people was going to see them. There was one at nearly every large station as well.

In the middle of the Circus on the steps of Eros there was the flower sellers. Not like the gypsies who try and push lavender on you nowadays, and then curse you if you won't buy, but ladies wearing long skirts and straw hats rather like Eliza Doolittles selling violets a lot of the time. Then it seems they just went. They were there before I went into prison one time and then they wasn't. They used to board up Eros on Boat Race night because someone was always trying to climb it. That was such a big thing when I was a kid. You had favours being sold for weeks before the race; little crossed oars painted in light or dark blue. People bought them but I don't suppose half of them knew what it was about until they saw it on the newsreel.

2

There's always silly girls going to run away from home up North, thinking they're going to be actresses. They end up on the streets working for a ponce who they think they're helping to get started in a business or something and then he'll marry them. The only business they're helping get started is his string of tarts. Then, of course, there's a lot of people who buy and sell women and use force to get them on the game.

Being a brass is a risky business. I was reading somewhere that the Albanian gangs who run prostitution along the Italian Riviera simply tip them out of a speeding car when they don't need them any more or if they're being uppity. It hasn't been as bad as that here, but there've been a lot of brasses killed in Soho. And some of their ponces for that matter.

When I was young there was an awful lot of talk about the white slave trade; talk of girls being given injections in the cinema or at a bus stop and next stop it's Argentina. I don't know how true it was. It seems to me it was one of those stories where you knew someone who knew someone whose cousin had been kidnapped, but it was never closer than that. They didn't need to drug these girls, just give them a good time and whoosh.

I suppose one of the first of the big ponces was in the 20s – Juan Antonio Castanar. Before him Eddie Manning, the black man, ran a few girls and some drugs but nothing big. The story is that Castanar had been a great tango dancer who'd danced with Pavlova but he found poncing easier. Who wouldn't? He opened a school for dance in Archer Street but it was just a front. He was what they called white-birding – selling women to dance troupes abroad at £50 a head. That was getting them out of the country. There was also a big market for bringing women in. He was also an arranger of marriages of convenience for foreign women who wanted to get an English passport. His great rival was Casimir Micheletti, an Algerian, who was known as the Assassin because he was so quick with a stiletto. They both ran strings of brasses and were real rivals. When Castanar was slashed across the face in the 43 Club in Old Compton Street it was common knowledge that Micheletti was the one who did it. Give Castanar credit, he stayed game and didn't grass him up.

There were a lot of French gangsters around in the 20s, some of them on the run from Paris where there was a real effort going on to clean out what were called Apaches. And Micheletti was fancied for the murder of another French ponce who went under the name of Martial le Chevalier, when he was found stabbed in Air Street.

There was another killing amongst the Soho foreign ponces in 1926 when Emile Berthier shot an Italian motor car dealer, Charles Ballada, in the Union Club in Frith Street. You can never tell what it was really all about, but one witness said that Berthier believed Ballada owed him money and just went up to him and shot him dead. Doesn't seem a good way of getting your money back to me. That's why money lenders will break your legs if you get behind but they don't often kill you. Unless there's got to be a serious example made of someone.

Berthier got as far as Newhaven, where he was nicked. He came from a family with problems up top. His father was said to have topped himself by throwing himself off a building at the Lyons exhibition in 1904. The jury found Berthier guilty but insane and he was sent back to France. Best place for him.

They slung both Micheletti and Castanar out in April 1929, but it seems like if you want to get back in the authorities can't stop you. It's the same with the Yardies today. Castanar was back within a few weeks but then he got chucked out permanently. The story is he was back being a tango dancer and running a small stable of brasses. Then in February 1930 Castanar met up again with Micheletti and later that night Castanar shot him dead. He tried some fanny about another man doing the shooting and then pushing the gun in his hand, but it was like those stories if you're caught with a bit of gear 'I bought it from a man in a pub. He'd got red hair and his name was Jim'. It didn't wear any better than that kind of story and he got sent to Devil's Island, which is where that American Eddie Guerin escaped from years earlier. Guerin rowed across the sea and was said to have eaten his mates who got out with him. Everyone looked twice at him after that. He was a good man with the vitriol as well. He'd done some big stuff in France at the turn of the century, but he ended up a sneak thief and shoplifter.

All that was when I was a kid, of course, but I was around at the time in January 1936 when another French ponce, Emil Allard, who was known as Max Kessel or Red Max, was found shot to bits under a hedge near St Albans. Only just starting to make my way, I was, of course. Allard was another friend of Micheletti, and whoever killed him took care to make sure he couldn't be identified all that easily.

Allard lived in James Street off Oxford Street and he was meant to be a diamond merchant, just like the Messina brothers were a few years later, but he'd been around over twenty years, selling off girls to the brothels in Buenos Aires. The more they dug up his past the more they found out. They eventually traced back his connection to the murder of a number of Soho prostitutes, including Josephine Martin, known as French Fifi, who'd been strangled with her own silk stockings in her Archer Street flat. She'd been a police informer as well as one of his little helpmates, who looked after the foreign brasses who were smuggled into this country.

Chief Inspector 'Nutty' Sharpe was the copper in charge and he was a right dodgy one for starters. He chased after my friend Ruby Sparks' girl, Lilian Goldstein, the one they called the Bobbed Haired Bandit, looking for Ruby after he got away from the Moor. After Sharpe retired he was mixed up in gambling with the Sabinis. He said he wasn't but he'd got a share in a bookmaking business in Thames Chambers, off Fleet Street. He was also a steward at Wimbledon dogs. The coppers tried to make him get out of it but he wouldn't. Give him credit for that.

Anyway he found out that Allard had been killed in a flat at 36 Little Newport Street just off the Charing Cross Road. It was one of the matching pieces of glass on the pavement that had led him to it. The tenant was a ponce, George Edward Lacroix alias Marcel Vernon, and the quarrel was all over a brass, Suzanne Bertrand. She was another who'd gone through a marriage with a drunken Englishman and never seen him again. Now she was working Soho streets. As Allard was dying he broke two panes of glass in the window with his forearm in an effort to attract attention and Sharpe matched up the pieces in the street. Lacroix and Suzanne got a car from a garage in Soho Square owned by another Frenchman, Pierre Alexandre, shoved Allard's body in the back and dumped it near St Albans.

By the time Sharpe caught up with them they had fled to France, but for some reason the French government wouldn't send them back. What they did was put them on trial there for Allard's murder. Alexandre gave evidence against Vernon about the car and that did him. He was sentenced to ten years' penal servitude and twenty years' banishment, which is a thing the French have always been keen on. They say you can't come back to the town where you committed the offence for so many years. Suzanne was acquitted but by then she'd spilled the beans about Vernon's partnership with Allard. Apparently they'd first met in Montreal and had worked the white slave trade together for years. The bust up had come over Suzanne. Vernon had left his wife in Paris in 1933 and gone to live with her and while he didn't mind sharing her, he didn't like sharing the profits.

That put an end to the French control of prostitution but from the middle of the 1930s, and with Eddie Manning dead in prison, after that it was the Malts all the way and they was led by the Messina brothers.

There's no doubt the Messinas give Billy Hill and Jack Spot money, but it was done in such a way that Hilly and Spot could pretend it wasn't money from prostitution. It would be money so they'd be allowed to open a club. The club never opened, of course, or if it did it would close just as quickly. With Hill and Spotty it was a question of shutting their eyes, although of course Aggie Hill had been a brass but that was looked on as years before and, although people said Gypsy Hill was a brass before she met Billy, she wasn't really, just a bit wild. The other story I've heard is that it was simply protection in Jack's case. He threatened to cut one of the brothers – who thought he was a pretty boy and a scar would do for him – if he didn't pay him a wage.

3

There was five of the Messinas: Carmelo, Alfredo, Salvatore, Attilio and Eugenio. Their father was really Italian. He went to Malta and helped out in one of the brothels there, learning the trade. He was bright; he made sure all the boys got a good education and, better still, he claimed Maltese citizenship. Then they went to Egypt where he set up a chain of brothels and got kicked out. They started coming to England on the back of the Maltese papers in the middle 1930s. Eugenio was the first and he came with his wife Colette, who was a French brass. He got girls over from the continent and then the rest of the family followed. You can't say they weren't shrewd because they bought up acres of property in the West End. Then it was a question of getting English girls on the game working for them. It was the usual thing – a good time for these inexperienced girls from the sticks then 'I'll marry you if you let me have it' and it worked. Girls didn't put it about then as they do today. The papers reckoned the Messinas were getting £1,000 a week by the end of the war.

It was a real business. The girls were under the control of another French brass, Marthe Watts, who'd had the sense to marry an Englishman. She'd been a working girl herself and she was totally loyal to the brothers. She met Eugenio in the Palm Beach Club in Wardour Street, which is the club where Hubby Distleman got it from Babe Mancini at the beginning of the war. She became his mistress and he had her back on the streets in minutes. They trusted her with everything and they was right to. She must have had chance after chance to turn them over but it never seems to have occurred to her or, more likely, at first, she never dared. And she had a hard time of it if you read her book – threats, beatings with an electric light flex was just part of it. But what does she do? She has herself tattooed over one of her bristols *Man of my life, Gino the Malt*. In French, of course. That's what I was told. I never saw it for myself.

You'd hear from time to time how the girls got treated by Eugenio. They couldn't go out on their own; they couldn't accept American servicemen as clients. I never understood why not. They weren't allowed to smoke, or to wear low cut dresses or even look at film magazines where the male stars were in any sort of undress. They didn't take off their clothes with the customers. There was also a ten minute rule. Punters were only allowed to stay that time before the maid knocked on the door. The other Messina brothers don't seem to have been so severe but they were just as keen on the ten minute rule as well.

They never reported for service during the war and Gino, who was good with his hands and who'd got a flat in Lowndes Square, built himself a hiding place in the form of a bookcase with a removable bottom shelf. Anyone who wanted to see him had to get by a whole series of fronts first.

You can never tell what they let the girls have, but it was meant to be around £50 a week, same as I got a bit later from my club, although they was pulling £100 a night, especially after the war. Of course someone was always going to put in a challenge to them and some other Malts had a go, saying they wanted a pound from each girl a day.

A pound a day was good money then, but it was worth not having a bit of acid in your face or a razor scar. Both of them put the punters off. Although Eugenio took off the fingers of one of the other Malts in Winchester Court over in South Kensington, the girls still went to the coppers. Of course they didn't say they were Messina girls, said they only knew of the Messinas as diamond merchants. A jury would laugh today but there was a bit of evidence that the coppers had been on watch in Burlington Gardens, off Piccadilly, when one of them shouted out to the girls, telling her to pay or she'd get a cut. There was a whole lot of stuff in the Malt's car, including a gun and a life-preserver as well as a knife. Three of them got four years apiece. But it was also the start of the end for Eugenio, who was done for GBH over the fingers.

He tried to get someone to smuggle him out of the country and offered £25,000 but there weren't any takers. He picked up three years for wounding. It was whilst he was in the nick doing that bird that I met him. Ponces are another lot you look at twice. Eugenio was all right and he had money, but you don't need to get too close. He got a fearful going over from Flip Hooper in Wandsworth when he tried to get flash. Flip was the younger of two brothers from the Elephant. Flip did a little post office in Rodney Road in 1943 and got three years, along with Spindles Jackson, and then Flip got something like eighteen months, so he was in Wandsworth with me and Eugenio.

Then another Messina brother went down. Just like the Sabinis did for their brother, Joe, when he got three years back in the 1920s. Carmelo tried to bribe a prison officer at Wandsworth for Eugenio. He picked up two months plus a £50 fine. But when he got out he got enough back; something like £700. The girls had been putting his share away for him and he bought himself a Roller. Now they were marked people and there was questions in Parliament about how they were getting their money. No one believed they was diamond merchants any longer. They'd also learned their lesson. No more knives. They just framed the opposition and girls who got out of line.

The man who brought them down was Duncan Webb in the *People* and it took him a while. It was the same Webb who'd go on and cause so much trouble for Jack Spot. Duncan was a funny man; in Hilly's pocket. He was a big RC and when he got a scoop in the days before there was news stories he'd put an ad on the front page of *The Times* saying thanks to St Jude.

He did it in 1950 – pictures and everything. The Messinas were on their bikes, or into the Rolls more like, over to France. Eugenio and Carmelo that is. They came back on false passports just like today.

Then off went Salvatore, leaving just Attilio and Alfredo. Attilio lived down in Surrey with a Rabina Torrance, a brass from Scotland – I heard her real name was Robina but I suppose Rabina was a bit more exotic. She was one of the girls who was used to frame a kid when the girl had tried to leave the family. As soon as Attilio cleared things up he was off to the continent as well. And then, like in that Agatha Christie story, there was one. Alfredo should have gone as well because he got nicked for poncing and for bribing a copper. He was another 'diamond merchant' and he'd said he'd no idea his 'wife' was on the game even though she'd run up over 100 convictions for tomming.

When she went out in the evening he thought it was to see a relative. It was a great shock to him to learn she was a brass. He had brought his personal fortune, some £30,000, to Britain at the beginning of the war and had dealt in diamonds since then. He'd got both diabetes and high blood pressure, which was why he didn't work. He'd never heard of his brothers living off brasses. He got two years' imprisonment concurrent on each of the charges, and a £500 fine – which wasn't much when you think what he was really worth. In fact Alfredo's 'wife' worked in the next door flat to his real wife, a Spanish woman, who worked under the name Marcelle and who was also on the game.

Marthe Watts took over the control of kids that Eugenio kept on sending over from the continent, where he'd been picking them up at tea-dances. She let them keep their own books and after every grand they earned they had the privilege of going to see to the big boss Eugenio in Paris. But the brothers just couldn't stay away. Attilio got caught next and was charged with living off Rabina Torrance. He had that Judah Binstock, who was later involved with the Victoria Sporting Club, as his brief at Bow Street, but it didn't do him any good at all because he got the maximum of six months.

They still continued. Attilio came out and went back to Rabina in Bourne End. She leased a couple of flats in London in her own name with payments for rent and rates being made through the Messinas' agents. Attilio, who was calling himself Maynard, had another flat in Shepherd's Market and the brothers had another one there as well. Deportation papers were served on him in 1953 but the Italian authorities wouldn't have him and, once the *People* had traced him, he moved to South London.

The brothers kept at it though. Eugenio bought 39 Curzon Street in Mayfair from a woman who ran it as a brothel for him. The coppers found £14,000 in a safe there when they did a raid. Then he decided he was coming back and got himself a couple of fake passports. Things were cracking up, though. Marthe Watts was getting on and her pipes weren't up to what they had been so she called it a day masterminding things and got permission to operate as an independent. After that Carmelo and Eugenio were nicked in a club on the Belgian coast and were charged with being in possession of firearms, having those false passports and procuring women for prostitution. The coppers found the title deeds to four West End properties, along with a report by good old Marthe which showed that one girl had earned £2,400 in six weeks. Eugenio got seven and Carmelo was let out with time served. There were the usual appeals and Carmelo got another ten months. But Carmelo was back over here by October 1958 and was found sitting in a car in Knightsbridge and arrested as an illegal immigrant. He received a six month sentence and was deported at the end. He didn't last long after that and died in Sicily that year.

Attilio had another girl working hard for him. He'd had her for about ten years, taught by that Rabina. Attilio knocked her about continually until she screwed up her courage and went home and to the coppers. He got sentenced to four years' imprisonment. It came out that she had earned between £50 and £150 a week over those ten years and had been allowed to keep £7 a week for herself.

Attilio and Eugenio went back to Italy. Salvatore lived in Switzerland and Alfredo, who by some good luck could claim British citizenship, died in Brentford in 1963. As far as I know the family was still paying rents on flats for tarts well after I went away over the Richardson thing at the end of the 1960s. I heard that Rabina had a son by Attilio who went into the church. She ended up with an antiques shop in Henley and she died in the early 1990s. The rest of them must all be long dead by now. I know their mother is buried in London.

4

As for the Palm Beach Club, like I said, that's where Babe Mancini stabbed Little Hubby Distleman in 1941. Albert was lucky over the case because he was charged with affray when Babe was topped for murder. Babe was one of the last of the Italians who was out and about, because Darby and some of the others including Bert Marsh, whose real name was Papa Pasquale, had all been interned down at Ascot racecourse. Now, what was happening was the Jewish geezers were taking over the Sabinis' clubs. Babe was the doorman at the Palm Beach in Wardour Street and there was trouble over quite a time. He'd thrown a man, Eddie Fleisher (called Fair Hair Eddie, got two years in 1946 and was in Lincoln Prison and Wandsworth with me in 1947), out a few weeks previous and now he was back. Babe went upstairs to see what was going on and he had Albert with him. There was a ruckus and Hubby Distleman, who was a ponce along with his brother, got stabbed. Albert was all for having a go and helping Babe but his elder brother, Victor, who they called Italian Jock, managed to grab him and hold him back. As a result Albert got chucked when the case come up at the Old Bailey. Victor was a likeable guy. He was no mug but he wasn't in the same class as Albert. Mind you he did right by him that day. He died a few years back, having been ill for some time with what I heard was cancer. Poor Babe, the Pros would have taken a plea to manslaughter.

5

Of course there was some smart restaurants in the time I was growing up. Not that I got into many of them, as a punter that is. The smartest must have been the Café Royal in Regent Street. Oscar Wilde used to go there and so did Lily Langtry. Before my time of course. It was about then that a man called Marius Martin got killed there. He was the night porter and it was obvious he was in the way of a robbery. Years later a man give himself up for it and they brought him down from Liverpool to London and charged him, but it soon became clear he was just one of those people that likes confessing. It's amazing how many people do.

Another was in a case down in Oxford after that actor Philip Yale Drew was done for the murder of a shopkeeper. He'd been a sort of Young Buffalo Bill at the Lyceum in the Strand, well before it became a dance hall, and then been in a real good melodrama called *The Monster* which ended up with the villain in the electric chair on stage. I say Drew got done in 1929 but that's not the right word, because although the coppers thought it was him, the jury at the inquest wouldn't name him and he walked free. A few weeks later a man called Dickens just walked into Glasgow Police Station and give himself up. It turned out he'd never even been in Oxford let alone killed the shopkeeper. As for Drew, he toured a bit longer in the play but then he started drinking more and more. No one would have him and he came and lived in Brixton for a time. I think he died in hospital in Lambeth. There was people who thought he killed the shopkeeper when he was drunk and couldn't remember what he done.

The first time I got taken out to a proper restaurant was by the Murrays, whose boy I saved from drowning. The Trocadero it was called, but everyone knew it as the Troc. It was in Shaftesbury Avenue and was a smart restaurant in its day. Smart but not all that expensive. If you was in there you could sometimes hear the fire engines from the fire station a bit further along Shaftesbury Avenue and people would rush out and watch them go the wrong way round Piccadilly Circus. Fat chance of them doing that nowadays.

The Murrays had style. They were before their time, coming out of Waterloo and going to a smart place like that. Tommy Murray, one of the brothers, was a sergeant rear gunner in the war and he was killed. Billy's son, who's also Billy, is still doing life for a murder up in Glasgow in a robbery which went wrong. Like an idiot he didn't come back to prison from home leave one time and that was it. Once they found him they banged him up again.

In the days when they took me out to dinners I used to help take the flowers to their stall on the forecourt of Charing Cross station. Billy and me would walk over Hungerford Bridge and up a little alley off Villiers Street with the boxes. Their mother, Phoebe her name was, had the stall. She'd buy the flowers the night before in Covent Garden and take them home with her for storage. The next day we'd cart them over. She was a wonderful woman, the cream.

It was in 1927, three or four years before I started taking the flowers down to her stall in Charing Cross, that someone went and left a body, or bits of it, in the left luggage office at the station there. I don't understand why they do it and then stay around because the smell's going to attract attention pretty quickly. All right if they've left for America but not otherwise. But over the years people have left bodies at railway stations up and down the country. There was one in Brighton in the 1940s, and that Tony Mancini kept his girlfriend in a trunk after he'd done her. He was lucky to get chucked and then he goes and tells a paper how he got away with it.

Anyway the body this time was a Minni Bonati, who'd left her husband who was an Italian waiter. She'd gone on the game and had picked up a John Robinson who was some sort of estate agent in Rochester Row – opposite the nick in fact. They found the man who'd sold the trunk, but what did for Robinson was that he'd left a cloth like from a bar in the trunk and a barmaid came forward and said that Robinson, who'd been a regular, hadn't been in to her bar since the time of the murder. Funnily enough they found him over my way at the Elephant. He said Minni had gone back with him to his office and there she'd cut up rough, wanting more money and screaming and shouting. He'd hit her to try and get her to shut up and she'd fallen and knocked her head on a chair. The Pros said he'd strangled her and he swung at Pentonville, which was where they topped anybody who'd killed someone north of the river.

Phoebe Murray's stall wasn't all that far from the Adelphi Theatre where there was a murder back in the 1890s. The very successful actor William Terriss was in a big melodrama, a thing called *Secret Service*, when he was stabbed by another actor who wasn't any good and was just jealous. They called him Mad Archie but his real name was Richard Prince. Just before Christmas 1897 Terriss had been playing poker in the Green Room Club in Maiden Lane where that restaurant Rules is. He was on his way to the stage door when Prince just rushed up out of a doorway and stabbed him. They put him away in Broadmoor where he lived happily ever after, appearing in all the productions. I suppose by their standards he wasn't a bad actor at all.

It was in the Strand that Nathan Goldberg, the guardsman, went mad and shot himself. That was a funny case, just a bit after the war. He lived down the East End and he thought people was after him so he killed a couple and then, when the coppers were closing in, he went and shot himself in a taxi.

At the bottom of Villiers Street there's Embankment Gardens, and one story has it that a woman ran up to a copper there saying a man had tried to rape her. She told him the man was still there and the copper wondered why he hadn't run off. Then when he went and looked he found out why. In them days women wore hats and hat pins and she'd pulled hers out and skewered the man's orchestras to his thigh. Serve him right.

I didn't get into the Savoy for years, although when my Jimmy, my nephew, got married in 1990 we had a good reception there with a lot of the families. In fact the Savoy didn't do poor Dennis Arif too much good in the long run. On 27 November 1990 he and a few others had ambushed a Securicor van with three-quarters of a million on board parked on a garage forecourt in Reigate, Surrey and, in turn, they'd been ambushed by the police. Mehmet Arif and his brother-in-law, Anthony Downer, had thrown down their guns, but when old-timer robber Kenny Baker had shot at the police they returned fire, killing him. Mehmet Arif pleaded guilty and Dennis ran the defence of duress, saying that Baker had threatened to shoot him if he did not repay some £60,000 of gambling debts. It didn't matter to Kenny, he was dead and he'd have been well pleased to help in any way he could. Duress is always difficult. You've got to show you were frightened you or your family was going to get it and, second, and this is the difficult bit, that you couldn't go to the coppers. The coppers found out they'd all been at that wedding together.

I don't suppose there's been a better murder in a hotel than the one in the Savoy in 1923 when that Mrs Fahmy shot her husband, who was some kind of Egyptian prince. Marshall Hall defended her and he made a wonderful job of it. She'd shot him in a thunderstorm in one of the corridors. Here was this poor terrified little Frenchwoman, evilly used because it come out she was waiting for an operation for piles since the prince had been putting it up her deaf and dumb. How could they convict her when all she'd been doing was protecting herself from this foreign beast? French didn't count as foreign. Later it came out she was a high-class Paris brass.

Eva and I used to put out a stall by the Savoy asking for a penny for the Guy before Bonfire Night. That was a place for touches. One of the doormen knew our parents and he wasn't that quick to chase us away. I go quite a bit nowadays. I like the River Room which overlooks the Thames. Of an evening there's a little band or a girl who plays a baby grand piano. You can even dance if you want to and it's not too dear either.

When I was young the papers was always running stories about people who disappeared and had never been seen again, or appealing for help in unsolved murder cases. The MP Victor Grayson was one of those who just disappeared. He was then the Labour MP for Colne Valley, good looking by all accounts and a spellbinding speaker. He'd been wounded in France in the First World War and had a disability pension.

In the autumn of 1920 he had booked himself into the Strand Palace Hotel almost opposite from the Savoy, went into the bar there and ordered a drink. Then said he'd be back in a moment, stepped out and was never seen again. He'd left all his luggage there as well. After his disappearance the pension was never collected. There was all sorts of stories about what happened to him.

The Troc, though, was a big enough stepping stone for the likes of me at the time, but an easier one was Lyons Corner House in Coventry Street. In fact one of the earlier jobs I had was in the Coventry Shoe Shop in Shaver's Place, next to what's now the Prince of Wales Theatre, just opposite the Corner House. That and the job at Boots were about the only two regular jobs I ever had and I was nicking blind from both of them. People were much more trusting in those days; straightlaced but trusting.

The Corner House had a band in a gallery and before the war you'd see every brass under the sun in there. The waitresses all wore smart little black dresses and were called nippys, presumably because they nipped in and out smartish to take the orders and get the food. That vicar from Norfolk, Harold Davidson, the Rector of Stiffkey, got himself into trouble over them back in 1934. A lot of them girls there were half brasses and he used to pop down during the week, when he should have been reading up for his sermon, to do a spot of reforming. Well, that's what he called it. It's like that joke 'Who wants to be saved?' 'I do'. 'Well, I'll save you 'til later'. It caused a great scandal because people complained and the church decided to defrock him. There was a long hearing with everything lovingly laid out in the Sunday papers, where else? Eventually they had him and they threw him out. Poor man, after that he went to do stunts in fairs and was in a bath of ice at Blackpool along with his daughter. He ended up on the seafront at Skegness putting his head in a lion's mouth and one day the lion shut it on him. There was another joke about him. 'What's the registration of the vicar's car?' 'RU 16'. I see his daughter died earlier this year.

The brasses would line up along Coventry Street. They were mostly Messina girls and each had their own bit of pavement and there'd be a real set-to if another girl, particularly a newcomer, took it whilst they were away doing their bit of business. Funny, they all wore hats and there they'd be scrapping it out and trying to keep their hats on so they looked ladylike at the same time.

6

Another really smart joint was the Café de Paris where the bandleader Ambrose used to play. It took a bomb in the war which killed a whole load of people. It re-opened after the war with top class people like Noel Coward and Marlene Dietrich.

Just about on the corner of Wardour Street and Coventry Street was Toliani's Latin Quarter, just where the Odeon cinema stands now. That was another nightclub and it was where Ronnie Knight's brother, David, got stabbed by Italian Tony Zomparelli after they went round to talk about a beating David had taken up in Islington. Zomparelli got four years for it, but when he come out Ronnie had him done by Nicky Gerard, Alf's son, and Maxie Piggott who also went by the name of George

Bradshaw. Zomparelli was shot in a pinball arcade, the Golden Goose, up the Wardour Street end of Old Compton Street. The name's been changed now.

Piggott turned out to be a real grass and put up Ronnie and Nicky's names but they got out of it. A few years later Nicky got shot dead by Tommy Hole, who was his cousin, and Tommy himself got done down in Beckton last year. Ronnie did five for receiving some of the money from the Security Express thing and then put it in his book that he'd bought the contract. Piggott was going to be a big supergrass like the others, but when the jury chucked Ronnie and Nicky out the authorities realised no one was going to believe him and they put him back in the nick. I've no idea what happened to him.

Ronnie Knight was one of those who had that A & R Club in Charing Cross Road which all the faces used. I'll never forget seeing Jimmy Logie, the brilliant Arsenal and Scotland forward, working there. He was a sort of potman. Later he managed to get a newspaper pitch just by the church in Piccadilly. Shows what sort of wages footballers got in them days. There was another man worked a pitch outside the big cinema, the London Pavilion, where the rock place is today. He'd got no nose, just a couple of holes in his face, but it didn't seem to put the customers off.

It was on the corner of Frith Street and Old Compton Street that Albert had his famous fight with Spot. He was in Mrs Bloom's greengrocer's when Spot came in after him. Mrs Bloom banged Spot over the head with the weighing pan and he staggered out into the barber's next door, which was where Albert used to go to get his hair cut. Bert Marsh put a moody knife in the gardens up the top of Frith. Then we let the coppers know where to find it.

If you walk along Old Compton Street towards Wardour Street, at the end on the left was the Two I's Coffee Bar which was famous in the 1950s. It was run by the wrestler

Paul Lincoln and his friend Ray Hunter, a couple of Aussies, genuine ones – not like the Yorkshireman Brian Glover who used to wrestle as Leon Arras the Surfboard King from Sydney before he went into films. At one time they had Tommy Steele's contract and he used to sing there in the coffee bar. It was the time when skiffle was all the rage and for half a crown you could sit there all evening and listen to people like the Vipers. When he was wrestling Paul was the real Doctor Death and Ray was one of the White Angels, and they wrestled each other up and down the countryside for years on end. So when they were away they'd leave a doorman in charge. A couple of nights in a row he found he was having trouble with some kids who thought they were being smart, and the next night they turned up they found Ray Hunter was the doorman. That quieted them down quick enough. Ray was very shy, lived in a flat the other side of the street just about over where a Chinese restaurant is now. It's well known that Ray and Paul sold Tommy's contract. Look where they'd be if they'd kept it. I knew Tommy's father, Darbo, well. He was a good man from South London. Not a villain, mind. At the end of the war he had barrows and then for a time he had the cloakroom concession in the Modernairre.

The club leader, Al Burnett, came on the scene during the war and he grew in stature as it was ending. I got on marvellous with him. He was another who liked a good villain. I did a bit of work for him now and then. Nothing in writing, of course, but when he needed help he knew where to go to. We had our machines in his joint. He owned the Pigalle in Piccadilly and you could get through cellars into another of his places, the Society in Jermyn Street. Faces owned or were behind almost all the clubs.

The Pigalle was where I had one of my coming out parties after the Spot slashing and it was where Billy Hill did Tony Mella with a bottle of Scotch when he was getting out of order the night they held a whip for Sully, who was a manager at the Astor. Arthur Helliwell, who had a sort of gossip column in the *People*, wrote it up. At least once a month he would write about Spot and the chaps, mainly Jack Spot. He never named names but everyone who was anyone all knew who he meant. People say there's all this interest today in criminals and there shouldn't be but there always has been.

The Pigalle was also the place where 'Scotch' Jack Buggy did a man called Reeder in 1961. Well, he did him on the pavement outside. They'd had a row when Buggy went to try and invite Shirley Bassey, who was the cabaret that night, to a private party. Reeder hit Jack over the head with a plate, which wasn't the most sensible thing, and they settled it on the pavement. Well Jack did because he shot him point-blank. He got chucked on attempted murder and picked up eight for GBH. Jack was an American really, but he was known as 'Scotch' because he worked for the firms up in Glasgow.

Tony Mella was a man I had a lot of dealings with. He was a game fighter, big man, but probably better on the cobbles than the ring. He fought a few times at the Mile End Arena. Buller Ward says a couple of his fights weren't straight, and when he came up against the Southern Area Champion, Mella got a good hiding. Him and me did a few jobs together. We took him up to Scotland once, more or less as an alibi. If we got stopped we was to say that he was a late substitute at the Kelvin Hall or somewhere like that, but fortunately it never came to it. Then, when the Carter family started quarrelling with Jimmy Brindle, my sister Eva's husband, and I had to take sides, I said to Tony who knew the brothers very well, that if he met them accidentally well, that was OK, but I wasn't going to stand for him seeing them on a regular basis. If that was the case him and me were going to fall out. He went on seeing them and I went round to his flat in Old Street in 1951 and I cut him to bits. Just as well he was a big strong man because if he hadn't been he might not have survived. He was very good though. He never nicked us nor did his wife and she could have done. She wasn't there when I did Tony. The police showed her a photograph of me as one of the likely men, but she didn't pick me out.

At one time Tony run a spinner at dog tracks. You don't see them much nowadays. It was a cross between a three card trick and a roulette wheel. You had to guess which way cards came, but like all the others it was fixed. There was what was called a Haley, a stick which was used to stop the wheel where the dealer wanted. Mella was a bit of a bully really. Mind you, he didn't always come out best. That little dwarf Royston Smith, who used to wrestle in dwarf tag matches as Fuzzy Kaye down the Metropolitan in the Edgware Road and was in Morton Fraser's Harmonica Gang, which was very popular in the 1950s, always said he'd striped Mella – which meant he'd cut him across the bum like noughts and crosses. At one time Royston had a club for dwarves in Gerrard Street near where Mella had a couple of his near beers. Mella went and said something out of turn and Royston cut him. I suppose his bum was all he could reach. I don't know if it was true, because I never saw it, but that was the story. Mind you, in his book Smith says Georgie Cornell come over to see me the night he was shot and I was running a North London firm.[1] I never did and I was in the nick when Georgie went, so Smith's not the most reliable.

One of the men Mella knocked about with was Big Alf Melvin, who'd got a good bit of form himself. They'd known each other from the days when Mella was boxing for Solomons, but Alf had retired from the game and was

---

[1] George Tremlett, *Muscleman of Soho*.

running a florist's. I suppose in a way I was partly responsible, because it was after I cut Mella that he got Alf to be his minder. He'd told the papers he'd been held down by six men whilst a psychopath (that was me) cut him a hundred times on the body and he pleaded for me not to touch his face. That was rubbish. There was just me. I didn't need six men to hold him down. Anyway, that's when he got Alf to back him up.

I don't know if he was a partner or what, but Mella treated him rotten in front of the girls and the punters. Mella had the club, the El Alabi, at one time and then he owned the Bus Stop (it was once called the Grill Club), which was a near-beer-cum-strip joint in Dean Street, with Melvin. Either that or Alf thought he should have had a share and Mella wasn't giving it to him. There was a number of different versions. Anyway one afternoon Melvin just pulls out a gun and shoots him. Out Tony staggers on the pavement and dies in the gutter with the girls all around him, whilst Alf sits in the club and turns the gun on himself.

Then a few days after Tony's death a young girl cuts her wrists. She'd been his protégé and he'd been trying to get her acting jobs, but people denied there was anything more in it.

At the inquests there were some letters read which looked as though Alf had just come to the end of his road and Mella had been a right dog to him. One was to his wife saying 'I came into this world with nothing and I'm going out with nothing' and there was another 'This bastard Tony Mella has used me in every shape and form. Sign here. Sign there and everything is down to you. I have been a drunken mug and how he has cashed in on my weakness'. There was talk that the killing was going to cause ructions in Soho but that never happened. In a way most people sided with Alf. He had a much better attended funeral than

Tony, whose wife was just a few weeks away from giving birth. Tony's buried in Manor Park Cemetery and Alf in Battersea.

7

The West End was nearly the downfall of my nephew Jimmy, who's now got the Tin Pan in Denmark Street, and it certainly was the downfall of that copper Challenor. He reckoned he was the scourge of criminals in Soho and he simply fitted them up. Eventually he fitted up the wrong man. He'd done well in the war and he was a riser in the police, but he was mad even before he joined the Met.

His finest hour came in September 1962 with his smashing of the 'protection racket' being run by Jimmy, along with Riccardo Pedrini, Joseph Oliva, John Ford and Alan Cheeseman. That's what Challenor said it was anyway. It was based on the evidence of a ponce, Wilfred Gardiner, who ran the two striptease clubs, the Phoenix and the Geisha in Old Compton Street. He said he'd had threats of damage to his car and that he'd be shot and how his car had been slashed. Then Riccardo and Alan were arrested outside the Phoenix Club by two of Challenor's aides. They were taken to Savile Row and told to put their belongings on a table. Alan was slapped and, so he said at the trial, Riccardo was taken into a cell and beaten. Both he and Alan had weapons planted on them. John, who had been involved in a long-standing quarrel with Gardiner, lived in the next block of flats to Pedrini; he got nicked and was charged with demanding money with menaces. The next thing, Joseph was arrested driving along Berwick Street and Challenor and two younger officers dragged him from his car. He was said to have a bottle of turpentine with a piece of torn up towel in the neck and a knife in his pocket. At the trial Challenor said he had information that Oliva intended to attack the Phoenix Club and Oliva was said to have remarked 'If I don't burn him someone else will'. Jimmy was arrested when he was pointed out to police officers by Gardiner and they said he had a knife. I don't think he even knew the others on more than a casual basis. He'd been given a lift by one of them once and after that it was guilt by association.

They were charged with conspiracy and demanding with menaces and went to the Bailey. Jimmy was acquitted of conspiracy but he went down for the knife, and the others were found guilty. Jimmy got fifteen months and the others between three and seven years, which was savage. And it wasn't until 1964 that their convictions was quashed by the Court of Appeal, by which time Challenor was in a spot of trouble himself.

After that Challenor didn't do himself any favours even by the standards of the times. There were a number of complaints, including one by the West Indies cricketer Harold Padmore, whose girlfriend Patricia Hawkins was running a near beer, the Boulevard Club, in Frith Street, when she got done for obtaining by false pretences. Padmore went to the West End Central police station to arrange her bail and, so he said, he was shown into a room with six or seven plain-clothes coppers along, together with Challenor who wanted to know, 'What does a black ponce like you want in a white police station?' Padmore told him, and Challenor replied, 'We'll have some fun with this coon'. The evidence at the inquiry was that Challenor made Padmore turn out his pockets and then hit him repeatedly saying, 'Take that black bastard out of my sight. I wish I was in South Africa. I'd have a nigger for breakfast every morning'. He then began to sing 'Bongo, bongo, bongo, I don't want to leave the Congo', a song which was all the rage at the time.

Padmore was then arrested and charged with obtaining money by false pretences and when he asked to see a solicitor was punched once again. The following day his solicitor applied for a summons for assault against Challenor, but the beak was on the copper's side and turned it down. The case against him, his girlfriend and another girl from the clip joint got thrown out and Padmore picked up damages of £750 for assault and false imprisonment – which I suppose wasn't all that bad, by the standards of the time.

Then Challenor must have totally lost his marbles because next he really picked the wrong man. It's easy to fit up the chaps, but not as easy to do it to political protestors and that's what he tried.

There was a demo outside Claridges in Brook Street when the Queen of Greece came on a visit in 1963 and she was staying there. It was all about the death of some Greek activist. One of the men who was arrested, Donald Roum, turned out to be a member of the National Council for Civil Liberties. Challenor give him a clip and said he'd found a brick in his pocket.

Roum was lucky. He had a good brief and, like I say, he hadn't any form. He was also lucky because he was kept in custody. He claimed the brick had never been in his pocket and because he'd been in the nick overnight he'd still been wearing the same jacket. He got some scientific evidence to show there was no dust and the lining wasn't scratched or anything like that. The beak threw it out but he still didn't get his costs.

But that was the end of Challenor. He was charged but it was found he was too ill to stand trial. Some of the other coppers with him got bits of bird though. Then there was an inquiry by a man who was later the judge at the Train Robbery and it was mostly a whitewash. No one seemed to have worried that Challenor stood and danced on the table or that he walked home to Kent every evening from West End Central. All in a day's work I suppose.

Joe Oliva had made a mess of things for himself. After Albert and Spot had their fight and I was away there was something of a vacancy in the West End and Joe put himself forward. Putting articles in newspapers is always the stupid thing to do but he went and did it, saying he was the new King of Soho and was called King Joe. When it came to the inquiry he said it was just talk and he got rubbished and it didn't help anyone.

8

Apart from spielers and drinkers there was plenty of up-market clubs as well. Bertie Green had the Astor just off Berkeley Square. Jimmy Nash was sometimes the doorman there, around the time there was a quarrel which ended up with Selwyn Cooney dead on the floor of the Pen Club, which was a drinker down in Spitalfields. The Astor opened after the war and you had a decent cabaret. That little fellow Davy Kaye, who was in *Those Magnificent Men in their Flying Machines* – he was one of the French team – was the cabaret a lot of the time. That was a hang-out for the right chaps of a Friday night. Verdi Wright was the compère and he used to sing of a night as well. Bert Wilkins, who's still alive and goes back to the Sabinis and is the uncle of Joe, had the Nightingale which, of course, was right in Berkeley Square. At the top, the Oxford Street end.

Then there was the Colony which faced onto the Square itself. That was one of the ones the Twins used to nip, and where George Raft was meant to be given an interest until he got deported as an undesirable.

Then there was Murray's Cabaret Club, just off Beak Street. Now it's called the Kabaret Klub but it hasn't changed. Marilyn had a party for the launch of her book *Gangster's Moll* there. Tiny little place it is. There was a postage stamp for a dance floor and minute lavatories. You could get a bit of food there. Christine Keeler and Mandy Rice-Davies worked in that club. I didn't go there a lot because it wasn't really for faces. It was considered a classy brasses' drum for punters.

The property man Peter Rachman was very big with Raymond Nash and they owned the El Condor Club together. He had a lot of fashionable clubs in Soho. One of them was La Discotheque in Wardour Street, where Mandy Rice-Davies became the manageress. One night, so the story goes, Ronnie Kray comes in and demands a drink and when she doesn't serve him quick enough he grabs her wrist so she slaps him. Rachman and Ronnie went into an office to sort it out and Rachman had to put up £5,000 so there wasn't any further trouble.

In Bond Street Harry Meadows and his brothers had the Celebrity and Churchill's clubs. Theirs were smart places, real upmarket; decent food, wine, cabaret and top class brasses. For a long time Meadows was a sort of King of the West End. Big man with a handlebar moustache like Jimmy Edwards had; always having his name in the papers about how he'd bought 1,000 ties or 1,000 toy poodles as Christmas presents; always smoking cigars. Mind you he had his ups and downs but, unlike us, when his clubs got done on licensing offences the beaks was on his side, saying things like how good he was in attracting the tourist trade and how it was a benefit to the country. But it was the same as with our clubs but on a larger scale, fashions changed. He had to borrow one and a half million from some Arab in 1975 and two years later the crash finally came in the November when him and his son, Andrew, and another man was done for living off immoral earnings. The Pros suggested that about 40 brasses worked out of the club. The judge, who was a former Pros himself, Sam Morton, said that whilst there might be clubs in London which were little short of brothels Churchill's was certainly not one of them. Not guilty, my Lord, for everyone I'm glad to say. But then a whole lot of waiters were laid off and they had to pay 19,000 quid to them. They'd gone on strike over a dispute about how tips were to be shared out. The club closed down in 1980. I think Harry was also under the cosh from some Malts. He went off to Majorca and his speedboat got blown up out there. I know he was very good in his old age to a brass who'd worked at the club and who had a son; he looked after her like a daughter until he died in the early 1980s.

Bruce Brace ran Winston's and that had the finest cabaret you could ever want to see. Danny La Rue and Barbara Windsor used to appear there when she was hardly out of the chorus, so to speak. Brace wouldn't give them a rise and that's when Danny opened his own club in Hanover Square. Jerry Callaghan, from the big family down our way who was a great pal of Alfie Gerard, had an interest in the Embassy. Another club in Bond Street was the Directors. This was quite a classy afternoon drum also. The girls would take the punters to a hotel since they didn't have flats like they do nowadays. The girls who worked there would know the punters would want something a bit special and they weren't just mugs. Then the Nash family opened the New Bagatelle which was just off Regent Street. That was a classy place too, you got a lot of out of town people coming for the evening, but I was away then.

9

There's not too many people get charged with murder twice. My friend Jimmy Essex was one, and he beat the charges both times. Then there was that fellow Walter Rowland up in Manchester, who killed his daughter and was reprieved and then got done for doing a brass. In his case there was some doubt, but there wasn't none about the man who did another girl near Shaftesbury Avenue.

New Compton Street is across the Charing Cross Road going into Long Acre. That's where she was found dead in October 1931. This time it was nothing to do with the French ponces. She just ran into the wrong person. Funnily the case involved a famous cricketer. The girl was called Norah Upchurch, she was just twenty and she turned up in an empty shop in the street. Her bag was missing. She was found by the manager of the firm of contractors who went to put up a sign on the premises. He got one of his workmen, Frederick Field, to break open the door.

There were a number of suspects in the case and one of them was a former England cricketer, Frank Foster. He'd got a funny story. It was the sort if I told it no one would believe me but he came out smelling like a gent. He'd been the last person to see the girl alive. He said he'd come out of Piccadilly Circus tube station and seen her holding on to the railings. She looked ill and he'd taken pity on her, invited her out for a meal. She'd seemed scared and wouldn't talk about things so he didn't like to leave her but went back to her gaff in Pimlico. There she begged him to stay the night and he'd sat up in an armchair with a couple of sticks handy, ready to give anyone who turned up a good hit over midwicket. Sure enough a man did come into the room, asked the girl if Foster was all right and then went off.

She'd been known to go to Chatham, where she was half-engaged to a sailor, and he was another suspect. Field identified a man who, he said, had borrowed the shop keys and never returned them and the coppers fancied Field as well. The coroner didn't like him one bit but there really wasn't no evidence and so the jury brought in a murder by persons unknown, which was about all they could do.

Then nothing happened for two years when, in the July, Field walked into a newspaper office and confessed. He wasn't the first and he certainly won't be the last. He'd had a deal with the paper at the time of the inquest: they was going to pay for his defence if there'd been a wilful murder against him at the inquest and then he'd give them the full SP for a series if he got a Not Guilty. There was no such thing as legal aid in them days and, unless you had a bit of dough or were one of the chaps and could rely on a whip, selling your story to the papers was about the only way a defendant could get a decent brief on a murder charge.

What Field said now was that he had met Norah Upchurch near where the Hippodrome is on the corner of Leicester Square. It used to be where they had that smart night place, the Talk of the Town. He'd gone with her to the shop but, although she had agreed to give him a plate, she wouldn't lie on the floor with him. He'd lost his temper and he'd strangled her. He said he'd sort of blacked out on the way home after he'd thrown her bag into a ditch near Sutton. I can't think what he thought he was doing confessing like that. The whole thing had gone quiet, but he said he wanted a bit more money from the paper to send back to his wife who'd gone to her folks in Cardiff.

The other thing is he must have thought he'd got away with the perfect murder and now he wanted everyone to know how clever he'd been. He'd been telling his mates at work but they wouldn't believe him. The newspaper sent a reporter and photographer to the ditch but it was dry and there was no handbag.

Of course, they put him on trial at the Bailey and once he'd thought it over he denied he had killed the girl. His explanation was that he wanted to clear his name as he had been offered a job in Ceylon on a tea plantation and when it had been learned he was involved in the Upchurch murder inquiry the offer had been withdrawn. The judge must have been going soft, because apart from saying that to confess to murder was a funny way of proving his innocence he just about told the jury to acquit. And that's what they did. He never went to Ceylon. He joined the RAF instead and deserted from them pretty quick.

Then in April 1936 they found the body of an old brass, Beatrice Sutton, well in her fifties she was, in her flat at Elmhurst Mansions, Clapham. She'd been suffocated with two pillows.

When the RAF got Field back he was put on a charge of larceny and he decided to have another go at confessing. Back to the Bailey and again he took it all back and ran a moody about hearing a quarrel and seeing a man leaving the flat. His story was that, on the run, he'd been sleeping the past few nights under the stairs in the building and had only gone into the flat when he saw the door was open. This time, though, the coppers had done their homework. They'd got detailed descriptions from him about what was in the flat and the type of injuries she had. The jury took only twenty minutes to convict him and he was topped at the end of June. They didn't hang around in them days.

Of course, if you get a serial killer he might choose any woman, straight or a brass, just like that man Gordon Cummins did in the war. It was in one of three air-raid shelters in Montague Place, a bit behind Oxford Street, that he did a 40-year-old schoolteacher in 1942. In a way she was a bit lucky, really, because after that Cummins started mutilating the girls as well. No one thought her death was anything like that of Evelyn Oatey who was strangled with a pair of silk stockings in her Wardour Street flat, just like Margaret Lowe, another brass, who got done in Gosfield Street just off Tottenham Court Road. Sometimes the papers referred to it as the Silk-Stocking Murders. Evelyn had been a Windmill girl and Cummins had got at her body with a tin-opener. He did another woman, Doris Jouannet, as well. She had a flat in Sussex Gardens in Paddington, which was always an area full of brasses, but she traded round Leicester Square. She must have taken him back to her flat because that was where her body was found. Then he tried to pick up a Greta Haywood near the Trocadero.

Anyway, this Greta Haywood was on her guard. They had a drink in the Troc and were on their way for another in the Captain's Cabin which was off Coventry Street. That's when he attacked her but she fought him off and, what did for him, he left his gas mask in her hands. She was able to describe him as an airman, and it was only a matter of time before the serial number on the gas mask was traced to him.

He'd still got one go left in him though. He picked up a Kathleen King, and took her in a cab back to her flat which was in Sussex Street, Paddington. When they got there he tried to strangle her but she yelled out and his bottle finally went. It wasn't long before they found where he'd been billeted in St John's Wood.

Just after the war a number of brasses got done and the coppers was never sure if their ponces had killed them or they were just unlucky with their choice of punter.

One of them was a girl, Margaret Cook, who was what they called an exotic dancer – which meant she took most of her clothes off behind a fan. She'd served a Borstal sentence and was found shot dead outside the Blue Lagoon Club in Carnaby Street which in 1946, when it happened, wasn't the fashionable place it is today. The police gave a description of who they wanted to interview but they never found anyone. They knew there were stories that her new boyfriend carried a gun but no one was ever nicked. Another girl who was killed around then was Frances Mizzi. She was found strangled in her flat in Poland Street just off Beak Street. After she died her husband got three months for living off her immoral earnings. No one ever got prossed over her death either.

Just about two years later, in September 1948, Rachel Fennick copped it in her flat in Broadwick Street. This time it wasn't a gun but a stiletto. She was found by a punter and she'd been stabbed in her back and chest. She'd married an American who'd gone and died in Paris, and she'd been a brass over twenty years and was getting on to run up 100 convictions of one sort or another. She was known as Red Rae or Ginger Rae. Rachel was a good-looking girl and she was well liked. She'd always hand out a shilling or so to a tramp and sweets to the kids, and she'd been really upset when her dog got run over. Butch it was called. She was quite a decent card player too.

What the coppers did know was that she had a friend who visited her more or less every weekend and he did the cooking for Sunday lunch. Although he denied it there's no real doubt he was her ponce. There's a story that she was a police informer and she was done either as revenge or to shut her mouth. Funnily one of the papers said she'd been done by someone left over from the Micheletti gang. It's difficult to know what that might mean. I suppose that the man and his mates were thinking of having a go at the Messinas, but I doubt it.

Brasses seemed to go on a long time in them days because that same month a sixty-year-old tart, Dora Freeman, who was known as Russian Dora, was stabbed to death in her flat in Long Acre in Covent Garden, which certainly wasn't the upmarket place it is now. If she owned it today she needn't have gone out brassing, she could have just let it out. She'd been on the game since as far back as 1910. There'd been a terrible fight and you'd think the neighbours would have heard but the wireless had been turned up loud by whoever killed her so they didn't hear her screaming. There was also stories that she was both an informer and a blackmailer. There's another story that it was Teddy Machin, who was once a Jack Spot man, who done the three of them. There's no way there was anything to do with sex if Teddy did do it. It would have been purely business.

10

Great Windmill Street has hardly changed except the place is full of strip clubs now. The place for the faces to be seen and be found was at Jack Solomon's gym at No 41. It was over the Nosherie and he had his offices there as well. There was a snooker hall in the same building and people just hung around there. I liked Jack much better than I liked Harry Levine, who really took over boxing from him. I don't know why. Jack liked a good villain and originally he was something of a Spot man but Hilly soon turned him round. I did a few bits of work for him; cut a couple of Americans, nothing too serious.

I was never much cop at snooker, or billiards for that matter, though I used to like to go to Thurston's off the Charing Cross Road of an afternoon when they were playing those long matches: Joe Davis and his brother Fred and John Pulman and Walter Lindrum. You'd get someone leading 64 frames to 43. Scores like that. Posh place it was and I found it very relaxing. That's long gone, of course. Ordinary snooker halls was where people often started their careers in crime. The halls was often over Burton's clothing shops. Out of work, scratching a living, go down to the hall and a bit of work might come to light. Maybe there'd be a lorry to help unload or even to drive. There'd be big betting on the top games in them places. People would bring their local player over and the money could run to a hundred easy, and sometimes up to a monkey. Snooker halls were the life blood of crime.

Then almost opposite Jack's was the Windmill Theatre where they had non-stop revues and the girls used to pose naked except for a few stars. They weren't allowed to move. It had been a cinema, the Palais de Luxe, and then in 1932 it was taken over by Vivian Van Damm who promoted speedway before the war. It opened at noon every weekday and it was so popular that soon there was half a dozen or more rivals. But the Windmill was the one that lasted. The place billed itself as 'We Never Closed', which they didn't all during the Blitz. The week of 7 September in 1940 there was 42 shows in the West End and the next week there was only the Windmill. Wags said it was 'We Never Clothed'. It was very popular with people on leave and more or less all our top comedians of my generation started as the comics there. There used to be a board outside of people who got their start there which was a roll call of honour. Dickie Murdoch, Kenneth More, Jimmy Edwards, and after the war most of the Goons, Harry Secombe, Peter Sellers, Michael Bentine, as well as Arthur English and Leslie West who was one of those memory men who could tell you who won the Boat Race in 1930 and the distance – you don't get them around now. They were just some. Of course there were a lot of others who you don't remember nowadays. There was Afrique, who was very popular when I was young. You see him in some of those old British comedies on the box in the afternoon.

It was good training because the punters weren't there to see them. They wanted to see the girls because your ordinary mug had probably never seen a woman undressed. He might not even have seen his wife without her nightdress on. Things were very different then; different manners.

I remember hearing of a poncing case at Sessions with a young lady barrister cross-examining the copper, who was saying he'd seen a girl take a man back to her room. In those days there wasn't really legal aid even for serious cases but if you'd got something like £2.50 in today's money you could get what they called a Dock Brief. All the old hacks who didn't have any work and the new kids would sit in court, hoping they'd be chosen by the defendant. Anyway the ponce chooses the young girl and the copper had said he had been watching from outside as the brass and her client had it off. Now it's her turn to cross-examine and this young barrister asks the officer how he could see in the dark. 'The light was on,' he says. 'Now, I know you're lying,' she says. And there's instant uproar because the ponce had got form and this sort of thing is going to let the judge put his character to the jury. 'Why do you say that Miss Smith?', or whatever her name was, asks the judge, trying to smooth things down. 'Because people don't do things like that,' she says. There's an uproar, with the defendant saying she's sacked and the judge realises it's hopeless and he says maybe there's a case in another court which she's better suited for. The Windmill's a lap dancing place nowadays.

At the Windmill the show lasted only about an hour and a half and they always had the Can Can, and then it started over again but, once you had a ticket, like the newsreels, you could stay and watch the show a couple of times. The jimmers used to clamber over the seats at the end of the performance to get nearer the front for the next time. It was quite a privilege to be a Windmill girl and you'd often see in the local papers how some young kid had been chosen and this was going to be the start of her stage career and she was going to be the next Vivien Leigh. There'd be some comment from the old woman who'd taught her tap dancing about how she practised since she could walk and how she knew she had a future, but I doubt many of the girls did make it to anything like the top. Not a few of them became brasses. Not all of them, of course, and not street brasses; half brasses more like.

The place all the faces went in those days was in a club on the ground floor in Denman Street, the Mazurka it was called. It was also known as Ginnie's Club after the woman who ran it and who'd been a Windmill girl herself; a lot of the girls from the show would get down there. Everybody used it until Aggie Hill opened her Cabinet Club in Gerrard Street. Halfway along it was, a lovely place. It was there that me and Slip Sullivan's brother-in-law had a straightener. Well, on the pavement outside – no one would think of having a fight in the club itself. Except when Hilly went and cut the man who'd been taking the piss out of Aggie's singing. She kept the club open when she went and opened the Modernairre in Greek Court. She left behind a man in charge, a guy from Southend, who was a very good driver. She had them both going at least until 1955 when I went away. Later the Modernairre got took over by a retired copper; Sandy his name was, and he called it Miranda's.

Great Windmill Street was where Climax Films oper-ated. It was run by Mick Muldoon who had a bodyguard, Gerry Hawley. Gerry was another face who ended up in Epping Forest in May 1969. It was all over blue movies. They'd been making porn films down in a flat in Bedford Hill, Balham, and they did really well for a time. I think the killing was over him trying to muscle in on Muldoon's business. Hawley was a real hard man, one of those who can take a car door off with his hands. He'd been getting a few quid for acting in the films and like so many he wanted a bit more. He wasn't killed there; it was in the Stockwell Road that he copped it. Then one night there'd been a big fight and that was when Hawley got stabbed. The Pros said he'd been stabbed with two weapons a total of 89 times, which was going it some. He'd been put in a car and driven out to the Forest. Funnily one of the films he'd been in was shot in the Forest. It was stuff for perverts; he'd strip off, run through the trees, chase this girl, catch her and then rape her.

Eventually Muldoon and his wife Sandra, who worked at Churchill's, and a kid with the unusual name of Kenneth Eighteen, who was her brother-in-law, got done for his murder. They said it was self-defence and that they was trying to stop Hawley from attacking Sandra but Muldoon got life. Sandra got a discharge but the kid picked up three years.

11

The first club I ever owned was in 1955 in Old Compton Street and I had a Malt front it for me. There was no way I was going to get a licence. It was a good earner. It depended on what it took, what I got out of it, but it was never less than £50 a week. I didn't have to put a penny in it; they was just happy to have me on the payroll.

Then years later Albert Dimes and me had a club with a fellow who owned a very fashionable restaurant. Again I didn't have to do anything, just show up of an evening so people could see who owned it and so they weren't going to cause no trouble. It was a classy joint, the Bonsoir in Gerrard Street, just about where Lee Ho Fook is today. It had a little band, food, everything. The fellow who had the restaurant had wanted Tommy McCarthy from the Log Cabin to go in with him but it hadn't worked. The thing with Albert and me was we was well known. Tommy, good man that he was, wasn't as well known in them days.

That did well for a time but it's the same with everything in Soho, all the clubs, all the restaurants; one day everyone's going there and tomorrow you're yesterday's dinner. That's what happened to ours. Also it was probably the wrong side of Shaftesbury Avenue. That bit hadn't become fashionable as Chinatown then and it was looked on as a bit grubby. Maybe we'd have done better if it was the other side.

Albert simply walked away. He didn't like staying out at night anyway and the place stayed open until half past two.

So Joe Wilkins, who was the nephew of Bert, came in with me for a time. But it was no good. We had to have a fire and that's where we was lucky. It took a while to get the place alight. In went the petrol and when we couldn't get a draught going we were smashing bottles of spirits to make what they call an accelerant. Eventually it did go up. It was comical really, but Joe worked hard at it, I'll give him that. Then we were lucky because we had that Bloom who'd done time back in the 30s but who was still working as an insurance assessor. Paid us out double quick. After that I went out of town for a bit. I had some trouble in Brighton and I was on the run, otherwise Joe and I were going to have a very smart little dive in Stratford Place off Oxford Street together.

The last place I had any real interest in was Charlie Chester's Casino in Archer Street when it was owned by a lovely Welshman who had clubs in Cardiff, Port Talbot and Southport. Charlie Chester, the comedian, was just the name. He'd look in at the beginning and shake hands with the punters. But Eddie Richardson and me looked after it for the Welshman after he'd had a bit of trouble with some local villains. He knew Bert Wilkins and he recommended us. We went there, discussed business and they were more than pleased to have our machines in as well. They were new then and they paid a decent weekly wage. At first we'd go in every night; let people know, but then it was just mostly on a Friday night for a drink. It was the presence that mattered. He was a good man, a really smashing fellow; paid me something all the time I was away after the Richardson trial.

Jack the Hat cut Timmy Hayes' son, Jackie, in the club. When we weren't there after the trouble at Mr Smith's Jackie Hayes was minding it for us. Jack came by thinking he might be on a pension but Jackie said it belonged to me and that was when the Hat cut him. Mind you McVitie was going well downhill by then. He wasn't the man he was when he attacked the Governor in Exeter with me, and it was only the fact that I'd been certified that saved us from another flogging in addition to the beating we got. The Home Secretary said it wasn't right to flog a man who'd been certified and it was a question of all of us got the Cat or none of us did. The place in Archer Street is shut now; closed about the end of 2000 and they've gone somewhere else.

12

If we were coming from across the river for a night out what we'd often do is stop and watch Ginger, the strong man who used to perform opposite the Garrick Theatre. I was there again the other day. Ginger's long gone but it seemed to be bigger than I remembered it. It's meant to be the other way around and things are supposed to get smaller as you get older. There were always pavement artists there – real ones not like us – people who did Leonardo's *Mona Lisa* and things. There was all sorts of acts – people who'd have musical spoons and who could play the 'Flight of the Bumble Bee' on a musical saw. You don't see them nowadays. There'd be bands who would keep on the move so they couldn't be done for blocking the pavement. But people liked them. We'd start off of an evening in Tommy McCarthy's Log Cabin which was the best place in the 1960s. You could buy anything in it; it was like a labour exchange for faces. People would come in and ask around if anyone wanted work the next day, and work would mean a pavement job or a bank. You'd think someone would lolly them but it never happened that I knew of. We'd get to the Log Cabin about seven, spend a couple of hours there and go on to Charlie Chester's and then about midnight go to the Astor. That wasn't a place for wives or regular girlfriends, though sometimes I'd take Doreen. She never really liked it because we was living in Hove and by the time we even got to the Astor the last train to Brighton had gone. You got straight people – racehorse trainers and the like – in there as well.

Going up Charing Cross Road from where Ginger used to do his act there's a series of little shops in alleyways and back doubles that lead to St Martin's Lane. It was in one of them, Cecil Court, that the shop assistant got stabbed to death in March 1961 and it was just about the first time they used an Identikit to trace the man who did it. It was one of those shops which sold antiques and curios like bayonets and daggers. They found the woman on the floor with two daggers stuck in her. They'd still got the price tickets on.

They talked to the man who owned the shop and he said there'd been a half Indian fellow in the day before who'd spent a lot of time looking at things but never buying nothing. He looked a bit shabby and came back later with a blonde girl and asked the price of a sword, which at £15 should have been well out of his reach.

Then the man opposite who had a gun shop said that an Indian fellow had been in the day of the murder saying he wanted to sell a sword which he'd paid fifteen quid for but he'd take a tenner. It seems like he had a Cockney voice as well. The fellow had left the sword and never come back for it. Anyway the coppers put together this Identikit of the fellow. A few days later the geezer's picked up walking along Old Compton Street with the blonde girl so they thought. She said she'd never been in the shop and she was telling the truth because it turned out to have been the fellow, Edwin Bush his name was, and his sister who was dark who'd been in the shop. It makes you worry about identification. In fact in his case there was a lot of evidence and he said the reason he'd killed the assistant was she'd called him a 'nigger', complaining that he was like all of them coming in the shop and then never buying anything. The judge said if that was true then it shouldn't have been a case for topping, but the jury reckoned it was just robbery and he swung.

Funnily Cecil Court was where that hooky MP, Mark Hewitson who was on Billy Hill's books, had a flat. Good man he was but foolish. He took a couple of half brasses he'd met in Aggie's back to his flat and they turned it over. Instead of doing the sensible thing and getting Bill or even Aggie to straighten it out he goes to the coppers. Of course the girls lollied him, the papers got hold of it and that was the end of him. He had to stand down at the next election. He just didn't understand that if you mix like that in our world you have to play by our rules.

Just up from Cecil Court in Little Newport Street was another club, the Premier. Any night of the week you could find coppers, chaps and the odd barrister or two, a few film stars on the way down; it was a right mix in there. It was the place where fixes could take place, where money changed hands. The owner was a funny old man who always wore carpet slippers.

There also used to be an escapologist who worked in Leicester Square by the Empire cinema. He'd be hand-cuffed and tied up in a sack with chains on the outside and he'd wriggle out in about half a minute. The usual way is to be a bit of a contortionist and be able to dislocate your shoulder so one of the chains comes off. Once you've got one off you, then the others just follow. The handcuffs would be those you give a bang to and they come apart. It seems a hard way to earn a living, for all he was getting was pennies and halfpennies and he'd have to have a bottler who'd also act as the barker with him.

His act wasn't far from what was one of the most notorious men's lavatories in London, just by the side of the green bit in the centre. No one who knew anything ever went down those steps. The police would have someone from it in Marlborough Street or Bow Street most weeks and sometimes it could be some straight mug who was down there having a jimmy when one of the poufs comes across and cops his joint. Wouldn't do him any good up before the beak.

There was one from that khazi ended up in Wandsworth with Dave Morbin and me doing half a stretch. What happens is a screw falls in love with him, and tells him when he gets out to go straight round to his quarters and he'll find a key and let himself in. Of course the pouf tells me and Dave and we didn't half have a laugh at the screw over it.

13

The escapologist wasn't really a conman but there was plenty of other cons going around. Really what the Americans call short cons – in and outs; no long-term planning required. There'd be people who'd have blue films – well they said they did – this was well before the porn business took off. It was really the corner game. They'd take a punter's money and send him round the corner to the second floor of some building and be well gone by the time he came down after he'd found there was nothing there. If the workers knew there was an empty room they'd send a whole lot of people, telling them the show would start in about fifteen minutes and they'd better pay now and go straight there so they got a good seat.

Another version of the corner game was the near beer joint. They were usually run by Malts. Girls stood outside getting the mug punters to come in and pay a few quid for lemonade which was worth a few pence in them days. Then a couple of girls would come over and they'd have to be bought drinks and probably given a few quid for their time as well. After that it was the hand on the thigh and a suggestion they'd meet later. Payment up front, of course. There was no question of the girl being allowed to go out with the punter from the club. The owner was 'far too strict' and of course there'd be an appointment at the clock at Charing Cross station or somewhere, and the punter would both do his dough and have a long cold wait before he twigged the girl wasn't coming to meet him. There was a big purge of them just before the World Cup in 1966 when Soho was going to be made safe for tourists. What had happened is that some kids on a night out had been swindled in a club in Lisle Street, which runs parallel with Coventry Street. Full of brasses it used to be. 'You'll always find a smile in Lisle Street' was the joke. Spring of 1966 it was. They'd been thrown out and found some rubbish in the street, poured petrol on it and threw it in the doorway of Number 23. Place went up and a man who'd gone in just to try and find a khazi choked on the smoke. The kids did the brave thing and went and owned up at the nick and they picked up threes and fours.

Nipper Read was in on the clean up before he tried to do the Twins over the Hideaway Club, which is what our Bonsoir had become.

I was in the nick over the Mr Smith's shooting when that fire happened but even before that I never had anything to do with near beers. They'd sprout up and shut down overnight. Most of the punters never went to the police because they'd be ashamed to admit having been in the place and doubly ashamed to admit they'd been conned. That's what the people who ran them relied on.

One of the troubles with going into Soho and going off with girls or boys is that you're open to blackmail. Much more when I was young than today of course, but there's still the worry that your wife isn't going to be too pleased to find you've been putting it about in strange places. One of the big blackmailers of the 1930s worked out of a caff in Lisle Street. He ran a real large racket blackmailing respectable people who'd got involved with a homosexual. Don't forget that in them days buggery was worth life imprisonment, whether the other geezer consented or not, and you could always expect at least a few months for being found plating some other fellow.

This man had it all going for him. One of his young men would form a relationship for a few weeks with a respectable person, in fact the more respectable the better. Someone like a vicar or a retired colonel, well they had more to lose. Then a bit after it had all ended a clergyman would turn up on the doorstep of the victim and explain how the young man in his past had seen the Light and wanted to go to Australia to make a new start in life. How about a small donation to help him forget about them disgusting things the colonel had done to him? And of course it always worked. They'd even have a little pray together when the cheque was handed over. Then down the drive out of sight and the clergyman would take off his dog collar and head back for the caff in Lisle Street. And once there was one cheque that was never going to be the end of it. Cheque after cheque until they'd bled the man dry or he screwed himself up and went to the coppers. The leader got ten years. He'd already done a five and started again within the month. When he wasn't blackmailing bummers he was into the white slave traffic, letting flats out to women. Having it both ways so to speak. The man had been an actor, which explained why he was so good playing the parson.

Much more down the scale of things there was the wallet or the fake ring which someone had found and didn't know the value. The mug is asked to put up a bit of money whilst a third person goes and gets it valued or, in the case of the wallet, puts it in the safe of a nearby hotel. The mug gets to hold the deposit slip, but when he goes to get the wallet then either he finds someone's been there first or that the wallet's stuffed with newspaper. It's all a question of greed. Some punter thinks he's getting something for nothing and he isn't as straight as he pretends or thinks he is. That's the only way the tricks can be worked.

The main racket on the streets then was the three card trick. It's been around for centuries. You think you can find the Queen of Spades and of course, even though you think the card's the one with the bent corner, it isn't. Even if you do choose correctly, and that's like winning the lottery, then one of the team will create a ruckus and the dealer will call the bets off. If you see anyone winning and think how easy it is, well they're just part of the team and the come-on. If you ever think you can beat them or it's a straight game then it's a question of think again. If you was ever in Bow Street or Marlborough Street where they used to bring them up you'd hear them asking for time to pay. The beaks had a standard reply: 'Yours is a cash business, and so is mine'. They knew the men would always have someone from the team in the public gallery ready to go down the fines office and get them out.

We always really looked down on these conmen and the three card tricksters. They weren't the cream. A lot of them liked to drink too much and weren't reliable and a lot of the others used to blow their dough in Albert's betting shop, A Barnett in Frith Street. Some did both. It's a club now.

From time to time I'd do a bit of work in Albert's shop and sometimes I'd be at the races with him. I've never been a betting man and Albert had to give me clear instructions what to do if I was putting money on for him. If Albert had a big bet you could take it the thing was a boat race. He'd had a top jockey straightened for years. I remember one day at the races Albert sends me to put some money on the nanny and there's a long queue. A chap comes up to me, well known he was. 'Don't you wait, Frank,' he says. 'I'll put the bet on for you'. But I was smart enough to say no. 'Thanks but no'. He knew I was doing a bit of running for Albert and he was just trying to find out the name of the horse.

WEST END

1

When I was young and in prison for the first few times, I heard about people who was legends even though they'd been dead for years. Everyone big, that is. You have to remember that the prison population was around 8,000, maybe 10,000 at the most (sometimes as low as 5 or 6,000) and everyone knew the stories of everyone else. They'd go on being told like you tell children bedtime stories. They love to hear them over and over again. Stinie Morrison was one they told stories about, and so was an American fellow called James Hynes. Hynes had run around with Legs Diamond in New York when they was bodyguards for that man known as Little Augie, Jacob Orgen. When Orgen copped it in New York in 1927 Hynes was shot four times in the stomach. He was taken to hospital and he must have thought that life wasn't going to get any better for him if he stayed, so he smuggled his way on board a cargo boat with a mate of his, Harry Kleintz, and come to London. So what he wants to do is put together a team and do a hold-up in Newcastle. Why he picks that place I don't know, but he couldn't get a team because no one wanted to know about guns. Use them on a robbery which goes wrong and it was a topping matter. Eventually he finds a few people who'll go along on the basis there's no guns. What they really wanted was a safe in a jeweller's shop. They're tunnelling in from next door when a couple of young coppers surprise them and get a beating for their pains. Three people got nicked but Hynes managed to get back to London where he was nicked as well. Then, you've got to hand it to him, he tries to get off the train back to Newcastle and leap from the footboard. It didn't work and both him and Kleintz got five years and deportation, but they got back in from France.

Next time he turns up is in November 1937 when he put together a wrap-up on a woman in Aldford House, Park Lane. Mildred Hesketh-Wright her name was, daughter of a millionaire, so he got that bit right. They tied up the maid and threatened her and then yelled out the house was on fire and kicked the woman's bedroom door in. They threatened her with an electric drill and she anted up the keys to the safe. They got away with £20,000 of jewellery and a bit of cash.

It was funny the way they traced Hynes and it shows how you should keep your gob shut. They found out who sold electric drills and the shopkeeper come out with the fact that the man who bought them had got an American accent and had been complaining about the weather. He also had said he was off to the Turkish baths. Someone put two and two together about how Hynes had been complaining in Parkhurst that there was no Turkish Baths when they had them in Elmina, the nick in New York, and even Sing Sing had steam baths. That was the place to get him – no chance of his having a machine gun under his towel. He came up in front of Goddard and asked for the Cat and a shorter sentence but Goddard wasn't doing no favours. Goddard said that the bullet wounds Hynes'd had when he was shot wouldn't allow it and he give him twelve years. At the time Hynes said he'd die in prison. He was right. He died in Parkhurst around the middle of April 1943. Couldn't stand English winters, I suppose.

Burlington Arcade was one place I never did. Never even tried; I just didn't fancy it. For a start all you was going to get was tom and that would only go for a third at best. It's the same with buying and selling straight. You want to buy and it's a very rare piece. Many people have fancied it.

Probably the Queen herself was looking in last week and she's still thinking about having it. Try and sell the same bit and if you get half what you paid an hour earlier you're doing well. 'No, there's some scratches and it's pretty common really'. Sometimes if it was hooky you'd more or less have to give it away. Then with something like Burlington Arcade you needed quite a bit of muscle. Including drivers, you'd probably really need to be five to eight handed, and where's the profit in that from a load of tom you might or might not get? Then there's the question of getting away. You'd have to run to one end or the other. There's no little alleyways in the middle. So you're either coming out just near Savile Row nick or into Piccadilly and think what the traffic's like there. You'd maybe need three drivers and three motors. If it went sweet you'd get in the first, but if it come to a right stoppo and you couldn't get to him then you'd have to try to make it to one of the others. You couldn't just rely on one. It seemed to me you was volunteering to get nicked.

Over the years some have tried it, though. The best one was when five men did the windows of the Goldsmiths and Silversmiths' Association in June 1954. They'd found a stolen Jaguar and people who saw them thought it was a film stunt. The car was found just round the corner in Carlton Gardens. They cleared something like £40,000 in stones but they'd have got nothing like that for them – at most, a third.

Look at that little George Enright, before my time but he was still being talked about. He'd been a jockey and a stuntman and he was another of those known as the Human Fly. He played a big part in the robbery of the Werner collection from Bath House on Piccadilly back in 1924, then took it all back because they couldn't find a buyer. It was like that Adam Worth who nicked the *Duchess of Devonshire*, the painting by Gainsborough, from

Askew's back in the 1880s. He could never find a buyer and eventually had to negotiate to give it back.

George picked up a lot of bird when he was nicked years later by Greeno when he tried to do an MP's house in Surrey in 1935. Whilst he was out he lived well. He had rooms in Jermyn Street and was a real man about town. I believe he'd done a bit of time in Sing Sing as well.[1]

Another who lived high off the hog was Robert Delaney whom they called Gussie, the burglar of the nobility. He was said to be the original Flannelfoot, but he wasn't. That was a man called Vicars. Delaney lived in Half Moon Street in Mayfair. Fabian of the Yard nicked him in a funny way. Gussie'd go out in rubber-soled evening shoes and the coppers reckoned he'd have to have them made special for him, so they toured the shoemakers in Jermyn Street and round there. According to Fabian he suddenly saw Gussie in the Range Bar, which was a smart joint off Piccadilly, and had him followed to 43 Half Moon Street. They kept on watching him and trailed him to Hatton Garden and then out to Southgate, where they found he'd been selling the jewellery from a series of raids. Gussie got three years and he was in and out of the nick from then on until he died in Parkhurst in December 1948. He was a brilliant climber and he'd got a lot of imitators. A couple of them died in falls, one fell on railings and another fell from a portico in St James'. He crawled about two miles before he died and they found £8,000 worth of tom on him from his final haul. I think it was the writer Edgar Wallace who coined the name Flannelfoot.

Old Johnny Hilton was another one who fancied having a go at Burlington Arcade and it was the end of him – just about literally. I first met him in 1959 in Wandsworth. I

[1] Edward Greeno, *War on the Underworld*. In the book Greeno uses a number of aliases for the characters and Enright is referred to as Reggie Scott.

96

was sent there just after Marwood was hanged at Pentonville, and me and some others put buttons in the locks on the cell doors. They changed the rules after that. Up till then everyone had to be out of their cells if there was a topping. Then everyone got locked in their cells until lunchtime.

The atmosphere in a prison was oppressive when there was a hanging. It didn't matter if it was a dog who'd killed a woman or a little child, it was still all over the prison. The screws were generally bouncy when there was a topping, it made them feel more important. The screws in the condemned cell came from another prison but when they went for their breaks screws from the local prison took over for a few minutes to relieve them. You'd know they'd been in from the important way they carried themselves, some would even boast about it to the cleaner. On the morning of a topping people would bang their doors just like they do in those American films and the screws would swallow it.

At Wandsworth the condemned cell was on the ground floor in E2 wing and there was a basement. Pentonville didn't have a basement. When you went outside, though, you could see there was a drop. Visitors to the condemned cell there would come through the double gates, then right and go up some stairs which let you into the man's visiting room.

One of the people who always turned up at a hanging was Mrs Violet Van der Elst. She started in 1935 when George Harvey was topped. He was a punter who had a row with a bookmaker over his winnings. On the day before the execution she tried to see the Home Secretary and claimed to have new evidence that Harvey had suffered brain damage at birth, but in them days she was on a loser. When he was topped at Pentonville in the March she arranged for a brass band to play the 'Death

March' and for 60 sandwichmen to parade with placards saying 'Stop Capital Punishment' and 'Mercy is Not Weakness'. From then on she appeared regularly at executions, arriving in her Rolls Royce, yelling at the crowd and throwing leaflets. She'd made her money out of cosmetics and she carried on for the better part of 30 years, being nicked for disorder regular. Some people thought she did more than anyone else to obtain the abolition of capital punishment, but there was others who thought she was turning the whole thing into a circus and they called her VD Elsie.

Anyway, Johnny Hilton was lucky not to get topped. He was doing a five. I knew him from working in the pouch shop and he wasn't a bad guy. Then again in 1966 I bumped into him in the nick when he was done with my friend Gus Thatcher. That's when he got life over the murder of a man in the Royal Arsenal Co-op in Mitcham. Johnny had gone up a league. I've written about Gus and the case before in Mad Frank's Diary. Then Johnny Hilton turns out to be a stone killer. He was out on licence in February 1978 and him and a feller, Alan Roberts, have a look at a Hatton Garden jeweller, Leo Grunhut. They fancy the job and follow him home to Golders Green but there it all goes wrong, and not only does Johnny shoot Grunhut but he also goes and shoots Roberts. He did the right thing, bundles him in the car and gets him to a garage in South London where he bleeds to death. It was a good haul, mind. Three grand in cash and near enough 300 grand in diamonds. So Johnny goes and buries Alan on a railway embankment down at Dartford, Kent.

Then in June 1981 he picked up fourteen years for seven robberies and a couple of conspiracies. It took him nine years before he was out this time, when he escaped from Kingston Prison which is now an old folks' nick near Portsmouth, and he did a jeweller's in Brighton. Then he and a friend tried their luck at Burlington Arcade. It worked all right for a minute, and the brothers who owned the shop handed over the better part of half a million in jewels, but when John left the shop the brothers ran out after him. He fired at them a few times, but you have to admit they was game and they got to him. By this time the police was involved and other jewellers was helping so Johnny was a bit outnumbered.

It was when he was waiting trial on the robbery that he confessed to the killing of Alan Roberts and the jeweller. The last I heard of him he was back in Brighton. He'll be in his seventies now. Killed three people, he did. I don't suppose he'll ever come out, I hope he does though.

Alfie Fraser – no relation – was another who didn't have any luck in the West End. He went down a couple of times for the same bank even though it was years apart. He did the Martins Bank in St James' Street in February 1955 and got over £23,000 from tunnelling through from next door. It was a great job, sheer artistry. It took them six hours or more because they come up against an iron grating they couldn't shift. Then they had a go at another wall and there was a place right up the top where they could pickaxe a hole they could squeeze through. They did that right enough and then they packed the safe with jelly and ran some wires into the street and blew it up from outside. That was just about the standard way to do it.

The trouble for Alfie was that there wasn't too many people in the country capable of doing such a skilled job: Eddie Chapman of course; Johnny Ramensky the Scot; Jimmy Boyle and Paddie Meehan; and maybe a few others. You didn't have to be Brain of Britain to work out who was in the nick at the time and look at who was left.

Alfie always said that Ted Greeno, the copper, fitted him up. It was easy in those days, particularly if you had a bit of form since you couldn't really challenge the police evidence. It gave them a licence for villainy. Greeno made out there was brick dust where they tunnelled through and there was the brick dust in Alfie's shoes. It didn't do Alfie no good at all to have a receipt which showed he'd bought the shoes after the robbery. Alfie always said Greeno took out the car carpet, put dust from the cellar on it and said 'That's how you got dust on your shoes'. He got ten years. Alfie did the tunnel, but that isn't the point is it? Greeno wrote up the case when he retired and published his book.[2] One good thing, though, is they managed to keep their car because the Pros couldn't prove it had been bought with the stolen money. They had to hand back a few grand, though.

When you think of all the successful raids there's been on jewellers it's the failures that stand out. The Aussie, Joe the Bash, whose real name was Leonard Davies, must have been the unluckiest I know of. Before the war he does a shop in the Haymarket and gets clean away, but just as he's getting in the car he spills the tom into the gutter. They didn't have time to pick it up and it's all lost to them. Then, twenty years later, he goes out with Teddy Gibbs, who got away when I picked up three for the stuff in Bedford. Same jeweller's as the one in the 1930s and again he gets clean away but this time a bus pulls in front of the car, passers-by start to have a go and they're nicked. Joe was 70 when that happened. He pulled a four and Teddy got eight years PD. They were giving them out like eyes were winking then.

Teddy Hughes is in Billy Hill's book *Boss of Britain's Underworld*. Bill refers to him as Teddy Oddlegs because he'd got a sort of a limp. Someone was asking me if I'd got a copy of Hilly's book the other day because people are willing to pay good money for it, it's so scarce. So if you

---

[2] Edward Greeno, *ibid*.

ever see one in a second-hand shop you should be on to a few quid.

It was Billy Hill who really started the smash and grab raids pre-war, him and Ruby Sparks. I think the first of Bill's was Carringtons, the big jeweller's in Piccadilly, in March 1940 and a couple of days later he followed up with a raid on Attenboroughs in Wardour Street. His idea was the car should go on to the pavement and so block the shop doorway. After that he did Phillips in Bond Street. He used a decoy car as well on that one. It had the number MUG 999 which, surprise surprise, the coppers discovered to be false plates. Billy did always like a joke.

There was another big raid on Carringtons back in 1965 when something like one and a half million worth of diamonds went. It was all a bit peculiar because the man who was done for conspiracy and receiving ten years later was Oliver Kenny, who owned the Horse and Groom, a pub in Brighton. He got bail, which was something, and he ended up involved in the trial of Reggie Dudley and Billy Maynard who were said to have killed Billy Moseley and cut up his body. The Pros said Kenny had nearly died of fright when someone showed him Billy's head in his pub. Bobby and Reggie got life and Kenny had a heart attack just before he was to go on trial for the jewellery. He'd been drinking something like twenty pints a day, so his wife told the inquest. The head eventually turned up in a khazi in Barnsbury.

I've said what a brilliant driver Danny Swain was but I think the best feat he ever pulled was in Jermyn Street at the end of the war. Him, Ginger Randall who was a good man in those days, and Jimmy Robson were trying to do a jeweller's when they come up against some Army officers. Of course a ruckus was meat and drink to the military and they got hold of Jimmy whilst Ginger was trying to hold them off from him with an iron bar. Danny just drove with two wheels on the pavement and somehow managed to catch hold of Jimmy and drag him away from the men. Jimmy scrambled in and in the confusion Ginger Randall got in as well. What a bit of driving.

A few people would steal jewellery and then sell it back to the jeweller, but now it's a dead art and jewellers are much more on their toes nowadays. It used to be very hard for an insurer not to believe jewellers, so if a claim was made there'd be a quick inquiry and then they'd cough up, but these days they go into things a lot more. As for art thefts that's really sold out unless you've got some crank who's going to put it in his cupboard and pull it out every Pancake Day. I've never been lucky enough to meet a millionaire who wants to keep the *Mona Lisa* in his cellar. There may be one or two, but your average thief isn't going to meet them. They're probably abroad as well. No one is going to touch it. The only way you'll get rid of it is at a car boot sale, if you're lucky.

It's much more likely to be an insurance job so you've got to know how to sell the stuff back to the insurance company. That's what Peter Scott, who was a brilliant burglar in his time, tried to do a few years back in 1997 and he came a cropper then. He was trying to help out Russell McVicar, John's son, whose position at the time was just about unhelpable. Russell went into the Lefevre Gallery in Bond Street and produced a gun before he walked off with a Picasso painting. Peter tried to negotiate its return but he ended up with three years. Russell was following in John's footsteps. He broke out of Kilburn Police Station and fell out of a tree, then whilst he was in St George's, Tooting, having his injuries treated, he managed to get past the security guard and he was away again. After that he did a series of robberies and I suppose it was just a matter of time before he got a pull.

Peter Scott's great mate was George 'Taters' Chatham. Taters, who was on Billy Hill's Eastcastle job, also did the Victoria and Albert in 1948 when he nicked the Duke of Wellington's swords, which he'd fancied for a long time. He didn't do anything useful with them though. He took the stones out and gave them to his girlfriends or used them as credit in spielers. Money just poured through his hands. He did the National Maritime Museum in Greenwich where he picked up Lord Nelson's hat. The jewels went the same way. He was still working when he was nearly 80. Poor George, he was a lovely man but he couldn't pick horses and he didn't play cards as well as he thought he did. He died back in 1997 with nothing to show for things.

2

If you walked along Piccadilly and turned right down towards Berkeley Square and then along into Curzon Street and into Shepherd's Market that was where the quality brasses used to work. Messina girls to a man. There was also a fair number of cards in shop windows for the girls who had flats of their own. There wasn't many in the 1950s because it was still difficult to get a telephone but these girls were the class end. The advertisements were discreet, a sort of code, not like the stuff you get in telephone boxes nowadays. Just things like 'Miss Macintosh gives riding lessons', 'Butterfly Needs Careful Mounting', 'Big Chest for Sale' and 'Miss Strict, ex-governess, will accept pupils'. There was a place, 43 Curzon Street, with a red neon sign saying 'French Lessons'. It was there for years and years. Eventually, for some reason, after the girl had left the police went in and found a whole lot of what they called equipment. They said they'd never even dreamed it was a vice girl's flat. They must have been the only ones who didn't.

3

It's funny, I've never been to the zoo in my life. My parents didn't have the money for treats that often. It was one thing to send Eva and me on a tram to Abbey Wood, which was a wood in them days, with a thermos of tea and sandwiches and our elder brother and sisters pleased to be playing mother and father, but it was another spending good money at something like the zoo. I suppose in a way since I've been locked up so much of my life I don't like seeing animals in cages either.

I'd have been coming up for seven, though, when one of the elephant keepers went and killed another. There'd been a lot in the papers when the man who was called Sandy Wee came over as a keeper with a special white elephant from Burma. It was the same later, when a panda came from China and when, after the war, that baby polar bear got born there and the papers ran a competition to name it. Brumas it got called – after its keepers I think. Anyway Sandy Wee stayed on and looked after the elephants, giving the kids rides whilst the head man who was Indian went home. It was good money because parents would always give the keeper something and he was getting about 30 bob a week. When the head man came back he wanted to take back this little earner and Sandy got sidelined. Of course, he didn't like it at all and he went and did the keeper. Well, that's what the jury found. Sandy said he'd been in the quarters with the keeper when four men had come in and attacked the Indian with a pick axe. He got a guilty, but they reprieved him and he was released and sent back to Burma inside four years so there must have been something which people didn't know about.

There've been a lot of good murders in the Regents Park area. By that I mean not simply straightforward ones. One of the best was that of Alice Hilda Middleton. She was shot by her lover Cecil Maltby in August 1922 and he kept her body for nearly five months in his flat above his tailor's shop in Park Road. Alice had been married to a seaman and she moved in with Maltby whilst her old man was away. Her husband seems to have known about her having it off and after he'd reported his wife missing the police went round to Maltby's shop in January the next year. Maltby called out of the window that she'd left him in the middle of August and he hadn't seen her since. There was also a terrific smell around the place.

The police then started keeping watch day and night and crowds gathered watching them. Finally the coppers got an order allowing the Medical Officer of Health into the flat on the grounds that the premises were insanitary. That was the moment Maltby topped himself, shot himself in the mouth. There she was, wrapped in a sheet in the bath in the kitchen. On her body there was a note, 'In memory of darling Pat, who committed suicide on 24th August 1922, 8.30 a.m.'

All around the flat were other notes he'd written, and there was one nailed to the bedroom door which said she'd killed herself, but no one believed it because she had been shot from behind. What was odd, though, was that the coroner thought Maltby was sane when he did himself.

It's funny how people like keeping bodies. That's what did for a man called Crossman. He was standing smoking a cigar in Kensal Rise, supervising the removal of what was left of his fifth wife, who was in a tin box and wrapped in cement, when the police come after him. He cut his throat as he was being chased down Ladysmith Road. The sixth wife had been living happily with him not knowing that Number 5 was under the same roof. It was the usual story: a neighbour complained about the smell and Crossman said he'd do something about it, but before he got round to it the neighbour went to the coppers. I suppose he was smoking the cigar to hide the smell. Back in 1904, that was.

Just after the war there was a big case when the lightning cartoonist Harry Michaelson was killed at his flat in Marylebone. He used to sleep with his window open and on Boxing Day 1948 a young fellow, Harry Lewis, saw it and jumped over the railings. Once he was in, Michaelson heard him and Lewis bashed him over the head with a metal chair. He'd never bothered to wipe off his prints from the chair and since he'd got form they was on file. The jury recommended mercy but it didn't do him no good. It's funny how some got reprieved and others who did exactly the same thing swung.

There was another funny case in 1956, the year I went down for slashing Spot. Ten years earlier a woman called Olive Nixon had been battered to death near where she lived in Park Village East, a small mews-like place just off the Marylebone Road. No robbery and no rape and no one ever got nicked – although funnily enough they fancied a copper, wrongly as it turned out – until a fellow, Adam Ogilvie, just walks into the nick and puts his hands up. It's like so many of these unsolved cases. Apart from DNA the coppers are just going to have to wait until they get a man for a traffic light and whilst they're taking his particulars he'll say 'I think I ought to tell you . . .' That's more or less what happened with Adam Ogilvie. He just volunteered it all. He said he'd been walking with a girl in the woods near Hampstead the previous Wednesday and he fancied killing her. And he thought he'd better give himself up, before he did another one. The only thing to do at his trial was like so many others – take it all back, and all that shows is you shouldn't open your trap in the first place. He was another who said he'd made his confession to prove his innocence because his wife had started suspecting him. Funnily, after he'd done Mrs Nixon, he'd gone up to a woman in Torquay from behind and bashed her with a brick. He got three years for that but no one had ever put two and two together. He and me were in the nick together. He was lucky. It was one of those times when Parliament was talking about stopping hanging altogether and for the moment no one was being topped.

There were a few more murders up that way about the same time which never got solved. There was Gladys Hanrahan who was found strangled on Cumberland Green. The cops fancied one of her friends she'd been drinking with, as they'd been seen having a row the morning she was done. The man produced an alibi to say he'd gone on impulse to Brighton but some witnesses said that they'd seen him in London. The coroner said that even if he'd been in London there wasn't anything to connect him with her death.

Then there was a brass known as Irish Kit whose real name was Kate Higgins. She was still on the game at the age of 70, so God alone knows what sort of punters she was drawing. She used to hang out in the Princess Alice in Acacia Road and she was found strangled in the grounds of Winfield House where that American heiress Barbara Hutton used to live.

The other case was Emily Armstrong, a lady who had a small dry cleaning business in High Street, St John's Wood. In those days shops closed during the lunchtime and that was when someone took a claw hammer to her. Whoever done it must have been covered in blood but in them days the High Street wasn't busy like it is today. No one ever came forward to identify the man.

A man they half fancied was John Allen, the Mad Parson who'd escaped from Broadmoor. He'd been a chef down in Burford in Gloucestershire and before the war he'd strangled the young daughter of some other people who worked in the hotel. There wasn't anything like sex in it. He was just annoyed that the little girl's mother had been put in charge of making cakes instead of him. He'd been in the nut-house twice before, so there wasn't any question of topping him and he went to Broadmoor. Then in 1947 he simply walked out. He was in the concert party they had and he was wearing a parson's collar, which is how he got the name. He stayed out for some years and got work, so when he finally got nicked and no one had ID'd him for the murders he went back to Broadmoor. That's where I met him. He was released not too long later and after one of Alfie Hinds' escapes the newspapers had him write a piece about how easy it was to stay out. He also wrote a book which was very popular for a bit. He'd be nearly 90 if he was alive now.

Poor Henry Jacoby wasn't as lucky as Ogilvie, or Allen for that matter, and he didn't have any social people to help him like Ronald True who got reprieved around the same time, as he swung the year I was born. Jacoby's mother had been a brass and when she had punters in she used to push the kid under the bed whilst she had it away on the top. Then he became the pantry boy in the Spencer Hotel, which was one of those residential-type hotels where old ladies played bridge, and probably still do for all I know. It used to be behind Selfridges in Portman Square. Jacoby hadn't been there three weeks when he decided to steal something from one of the rooms in the middle of the night. He opened the door of the room of a Lady White, and when she screamed he hit her with a hammer he'd taken from a toolbag. He washed the hammer and put it back in the bag and went back to bed. He might have got away with it because the police thought it was an outside job but eventually he went and confessed.

His brief suggested that he'd been given the third degree by the coppers – which was about all that he could suggest – but the judge, McCardie, wasn't having it and said 'What is the First Degree?' The jury recommended mercy and there was a campaign for a reprieve because he was only eighteen but it didn't do him any good. He still got topped. Some people also brought up a campaign to have his body buried outside the prison but that didn't work either. It was there when I was in after the war. Just a number in the wall for him: H.J. 382.

As it happened, a few years later in 1932 the judge topped himself. He did it in his flat in St James', shot himself. Just as well he was successful because, if he hadn't, he could have been charged with the offence of attempted suicide. Only crime that I know when the attempt was punished and the crime itself wasn't. There was all sorts of stories about why he did himself, but it seems like he was in the hands of the moneylenders. Big gambler – and you know what happens with them ninety-nine per cent of the time. It was also said he had a Jewish mistress, which wouldn't have gone down too well in society. He was never seen with her in public. She used to go up the back steps to his flat so the porters never saw her. Of course, it was all put down to overwork, service of the country, all that sort of rubbish.

The last time the police came to see me over a murder was when that businessman Donald Urquhart, who had owned the Elstree Golf Club, got himself killed in Marylebone High Street in a drive-by shooting. The guy had been having dinner in this restaurant with his girlfriend and was on his way home with his girlfriend to the block of flats where old Bert Wilkins – who was with the Sabinis and the uncle of my friend Joe – had lived, when he got shot. A man pulled up on a motorbike and did him twice in the nut. Then a bit later that year this fellow, Tommy Roche, who'd been working on the M4 down near Heathrow, was shot in another drive-by. Someone took him out from the back of a motorbike.

Anyone who's been searched regular will know when the coppers are serious. That's when the light fittings get unscrewed, the wallpaper comes off and the floorboards come up. Then there's the ones which are more for show and this was one of them. Marilyn and me were living in Duncan Street in the Angel at the time and they just turned up with a warrant saying they were looking for charlie. Of course there wasn't any and that's when they said they were from the Murder Squad and were wanting to talk about Urquhart. I told them I'd never heard of him and I hadn't.

As for Tommy Roche, apparently he'd done a bit of work for Urquhart and he'd been a hanger-on of the Twins so I suppose there was reason to think at least I knew him but, in fact, I didn't. I'd have been older even than Johnny Hilton if I'd done it. I never fancied motorbikes at all, and getting on the back of them at the age of 71 would have been a bit much. I don't think I've ever been on the back of one in my life and I've certainly never driven one. The coppers were very pleasant; we had a cup of tea but then they went and took my address book – and just on ten years later I've still never had it back.

There was all sorts of stories as to who had done Urquhart. No one ever thought that the shooter was anything but a contract, but it was the why that was interesting. A report in the papers said it had cost £20,000 and that it was all over drugs and, in fairness, that was the way it looked at first. But when it come to it, it wasn't. It was just a simple business deal which had gone wrong and the loser wanted something done about it.

Graeme West was the guy who actually did it and he couldn't have advertised himself much better. As well as telling people, he'd done just about everything else wrong. He'd been seen around the golf club and he'd got Urquhart's ex-directory number on his mobile. Not only that but he'd left his BMW near Urquhart's flat and when he comes back it had been clamped. If that's not enough his van had been given a parking ticket in Marylebone as well. What is it those advertisements say? It pays to advertise.

It seems the figure was £20,000 but no one has ever been prossed for putting out the contract. The story is that it's a solicitor who has been on his toes ever since. If it is, he won't be the only solicitor who's been suspected of organising a killing.

You might think nothing happened in that bit of town but you'd be wrong. Bickenhall Mansions was where those Russians, Ruslan and Nazarbek Outsiev, got done way back in 1993. Ruslan fancied himself as the Prime Minister of Chechnya and the pair was pouring money around the clubs like it was water, spending other people's money on the brasses. Both of them shot in the head. One of the men who did it topped himself in Belmarsh and the other got life.

4

I suppose in my time there's been two really big events in Knightsbridge and one of them was the Spaghetti House siege, which lasted five days in September 1975. Of course in those days it was before terrorism and those embassy sieges. The guys who got done for it claimed it was political, a strike for Black Power, but really I think it was over money. That wrestler, Norbert Rondel, got done for putting up the job and supplying the guns but Norbert denied it all and I'm pleased to say he got chucked.

What the Pros said was that Norbert ran a gambling club, the Apartment in Rupert Street, and he was owed money by a punter, Lino Termine, who'd worked at the Spaghetti House and knew that every Saturday evening the managers from the other branches in London come round with the week's takings. He put the job up to clear his debt. Well, that's what the Pros said anyway. It was going to be a straight blag but one of the managers escaped and rang the police, who was round in a minute. The response time was better in them days. And that's when it all came on top and Frank Davies, who was leading the whole thing, and the others took the rest hostages. They said they was only coming out in an aeroplane or a coffin but eventually they surrendered. The only one who was hurt was Frankie, who shot himself accidentally when it was nearly all over. It seems that by the end there was one of those situations between the hostages and the men where they congratulated each other that they'd survived. Frank, who'd done a previous ten for a blag in North London, picked up 21 and the others a few years less. As I say, Norbert got chucked and there was a picture of him in the papers standing on his head to celebrate. I think he'd lost his club with the eight months he was in the nick on remand, though. Termine pleaded guilty and got a six.

Norbert went on to have clubs in Bayswater. He's still alive and was dealing in cars in the Borough the last I heard of him. He come over before the war as a refugee so he's got to be my age and more.

The second big thing was the blag organised by Valerio Viccei from the Knightsbridge Safe Deposit Centre. His book said he cleared £60 million, but who can tell? I don't think anybody ever knew how much really went. If it goes from one of the boxes people aren't really in a position to tell the coppers they've had a £100,000 in notes locked away from the taxman are they?

Viccei's father was a lawyer back in Italy but the boy was wild. He was on the run from Italy and he'd already done a blag at Coutts, where he'd got bitten by a cashier, before he thought of the Knightsbridge job. He did a second job and that picked him up nearly £50,000 and then he did £70,000 in travellers' cheques from the American Express in Mayfair, so you could say he was big time.

What he did next was to latch on to a fellow, Parvez Latif, who was the manager of the safe deposit. He took him out to places like Tramps and wined and dined and charlie'd him to persuade him to be part of a phoney tie-up job. The man was to let him and some others into the Centre and switch off the closed circuit telly. He was also supposed to point out the best boxes. In return he was going to get a fabulous pay out. It would be running down his nose. The guards at the Centre weren't in on it and they had to be overpowered. The first mistake Valerio made was to cut himself whilst he was opening one of the boxes and leave blood and fingerprints all over the place. After that it was just a matter of time. One of the others was staying in White's Hotel in Hyde Park and he was watched. The coppers soon found out that Viccei was visiting him and he got a pull in a traffic jam at Marble Arch. One of the members of the team, Steve Mann, turned grass and got a five whilst poor old Latif drew an eighteen. The others got bits in between. Valerio picked up a 22, but by 1993 he'd been sent back to Italy. He'd always boasted that was what was going to happen. I see he died in a shoot-out with the coppers there a couple of years back. He was game to the last. Him and his mate had some carnival masks and the coppers thought he was going to do another bank.

5

Victoria's never had the happiest memories for me. It's where I had a bull with that judge, Lawton, on the platform when I was with Doreen waiting for the train to go home to Brighton. I was really giving it to him and shouting, telling him what a dog his father had been as a screw, when Doreen pulled me away. Years later in the Torture Trial I wanted my counsel to object to Lawton being the judge, saying that he'd had this row with me and it wouldn't look like he was unbiased. At first Lawton denied he'd ever seen me and then a bit later he swallowed it and said, well yes, there had been an incident with a drunken man, but he'd clear forgot it and it wouldn't prejudice him or me. And everyone said 'Of course not, My Lord' and that was that.

Not that I haven't had some touches in the area. Back in the November of 1944 me and Patsy Lyons and another man did the jeweller's in the courtway from Victoria Street to Caxton Street. It was one of a series of shops. You couldn't get a car up the alleyway. Me and the other man, who got Borstal, we went in the jeweller's and held them up with a bar of iron. I started smashing the display counter and we cleared about £12,000 from the window. All the people came running out and seeing as how it was wartime, with all these soldiers and airmen and sailors about, those were the 'have a go' days. Not like today when that poor woman who got killed at Euston trying to get her handbag back seems to have been blamed for trying. People should shout for help and not have a go themselves, some spokesman said. It wasn't like that in the 1940s.

We were on our toes at once and got clean away in the car back to Bermondsey. It was when we tried to fence it that we found out there wasn't as much as we'd hoped. I know it sounds good money, but £12,000 of tom is going to come down to three for a quick sale and that means a grand each at best. So we decided to do another jeweller's in Bond Street. Stark raving mad we was, using the same car. Someone had obviously taken the number and the coppers were looking for us. We was going through the Rotherhithe Tunnel to work our way through to the West End when the police cars came after us. We got out of the tunnel, which was the main thing, but at the junction of Old Street and City Road we was hemmed in and crashed. We all jumped out and made a run for it. I ran behind a bus, stopped, took off my gloves and scarf and just turned round and walked along back towards the police. The police thought I'd run straight on and I got clean away. Poor Patsy got five years' penal servitude.

Wilton Road just by Victoria Station was where the first conviction in the world came from a glove print. Fingerprints was one thing and later came palm prints, but it wasn't until 1975 that a fellow got caught through a glove. He'd done a surveyor's. The Pros said that police laboratory tests showed that 'the chances of finding matching gloves were the same as one man's fingerprints matching another and that, as is well known, is virtually nil' and he went and pleaded guilty. So that was the end of wearing gloves if you're caught with them on you.

I think it was about that time that the Biograph cinema in Wilton Road next to Victoria Station closed. It was a real gobbler's gulch, a rundown fleapit of a place where the punters never even pretended they was watching the film. There was a constant stream of men going to the lavatories. You'd ruin your trousers rather than go in the khazi there. Of course the coppers kept watch on it and it kept getting raided. You'd have thought men would have learned not to go in.

TOTTENHAM COURT ROAD

1

The best robbery there's been – and that's not knocking them on the Great Train – was Billy Hill's Eastcastle Street Post Office job in 1952. That was where a car was driven across a post office van. Once they got the money out they moved it from place to place in London until it was safe. The reasons I say it was the best is that the coppers never got the money back and no one got done for it. The money, with inflation, must have been about what they got for the Train, certainly what they kept. The other thing was it actually taught the coppers how to do their job. Not that they learned.

What Billy was keen on was security. He didn't want anyone lollying him by mistake or being evil, so when he decided the job was on he had all his team in his flat and locked them up until it was time to go. Yet a few years later when that copper Bert Wickstead, who liked being called the Fox, was doing a raid on the vice haunts in Soho he made the mistake of letting it be known what was on, and as a result all the birds had flown by the time he came looking for them. He didn't make the same mistake twice and neither did Nipper Read when he went for the Twins. I read Wickstead died in March this year. I never knew him, thank the Lord. Even other coppers acknowledged he was a king fit-up merchant.

What I can't emphasise enough is how security-con-scious and clever Bill was. The trouble with jobs is that the more people on them the bigger the chance there is of a leak. In a way Bill was lucky. The London Airport job, which Jack Spot organised, must have had about twelve men on it and the chances of a leak just multiply. People are bound to tell their wives or girlfriends something's going off, and they tell their mothers and then it's all over London and someone's going to grass. The best job is if there's only one of you. With the Eastcastle job Bill didn't really have to tell too many people exactly what was going to happen or when. He was lucky in so far as he'd got Billy Benstead, who was one of the men who got away from the airport, on the job. So he could say, 'Look what happened when too many people knew about that job'. And Billy Benstead could back him up and say 'Bill's right'.

One of the men on the raid was Terry Hogan. He was a good man who only ever did a bit of bird and nothing to do with the blaggings he was on. Then he give it all up in the 1960s, married and left crime altogether. He died in the middle 1990s.

A few years later, in March 1961, there was another robbery in Maple Place near Eastcastle Street but this time it wasn't anywhere nearly as successful as Bill's. In fact there was a lot of bird handed out over it. Someone had grassed even before it got underway. It was on a firm of building contractors and the coppers got on to a man, Henry Jeffery, whose van they spotted in the neighbourhood. He'd just finished a six and was looking for work. They knew he was linked up with Tony Terroni from a very good family. When it came to it the whole thing was a ready-eye. The coppers got the driver straight away and they knew where to look for the rest. By today's standards, and given firearms was used, the sentencing wasn't that bad. The seven of them got 46 years between them. It would be about double that today, if not more.

Down just by New Oxford Street there used to be the Horseshoe Hotel and there was a big killing there back in 1913. An Armenian shot and killed the manageress, and newspaper vendor John Starchfield, who had a pitch just on the corner, got in the way and cut off his escape. He got shot in the stomach and was given £50 and a quid a week pension. That year he was the hero. But the next year he was the villain when his seven-year-old boy, Willie, was found dead in a train at Shoreditch. The train had come from Chalk Farm and when another kid got on at Mildmay Park he saw Willie under the seat. He'd been strangled and his teeth had been loosened, which sounds to me as if someone had tried to get him to plate them.

Apparently his mother said she'd sent him out on an errand to a shop a couple of hundred yards away, and it was a mystery how he ended up on the train. Anyway they interviewed Dad and he told them he'd been in bed at the time and a hotel porter confirmed it. Then that hooky man who run *John Bull* and ended up doing time himself, Horatio Bottomley, put up a reward of £500 and of course all the grasses came out looking for it. A man called Moore said he'd seen the Starchfields together in Endell Street in Covent Garden, where they later had the clap hospital, around three-thirty the afternoon the boy was done. John Starchfield then got arrested and things got worse for him when a signalman said he'd seen a pair who looked like the Starchfields as the train went past and the man had been leaning over the boy. That did for him. The inquest jury said it was murder and Starchfield went up to the Bailey.

Things did get better, however. Moore, the man who'd put Starchfield's name in the frame, tried to commit suicide. Then the judge said he didn't think the ID evidence was strong enough and he told the DPP to throw the case out. John Starchfield didn't last long, though, because he died a couple of years later from the injuries he'd received when he'd been a hero. A lot of people always said he had done his son in, but why? I'd go along with his meeting a maniac.

Just behind the old Dominion Cinema – where Totten-ham Court Road meets New Oxford Street and the Charing Cross Road – was where Jack Spot did the reporter Duncan Webb. He had him set up with a fake call and started bashing him about in an alleyway, Bainbridge Street. Webb falls to the ground and breaks his arm. He prossed Spot and then sued him in the local county court. He said he'd lost a whole lot of money through not being able to type and he'd had to hire a secretary so he could finish a book. He got a bit over £700. Duncan was a good-looking man, a lot of wavy hair, smoked a pipe like so many did then. I liked him. He come to see me on a visit in Birmingham once and he gave me a gee when I was locked up, awaiting the Cat, when I did the governor in Exeter.

Eddie Richardson and me had Atlantic Machines in Windmill Street. That was just opposite Store Street where they had the Court of Protection which looked after the estates of nutters. It's funny how the law gives protection but when we do it it's an offence. At first we just had one shop but then we took the one next door as well. Leslie McCarthy was really the office manager and he kept things running properly. He was Bert McCarthy, the boxing promoter's, brother. One time Bert had Frank Bruno on his books. There was dozens of McCarthys and they all seemed to be half related to each other in one way or another. Sammy McCarthy, who was also a boxer before he got done for armed robbery, was a cousin of some sort. Those were good days, things was running well and it was being run straight. As I've said, when we was all nicked over the Torture Trial the coppers went round the country trying to find someone who would say we'd been running Atlantic as a long firm, but they never could.

We'd begun at the right time getting the one-armed bandits from America through Hilly and Albert's connec-tions. We were trying to build it up and we just took our

Above Ron and
Reggie Kray with
their mother, Vi

Right Jack 'Spot'.
I told him it was on
and it was

Left Double spy, George Blake. This picture was issued by Scotland Yard after his escape from Wormwood Scrubs prison, West London in 1966. He seemed a cut above us, I suppose he was

Below Ruth Ellis. She'd probably have got probation today

andy Rice-Davies leaving the Old Bailey. A tough girl – she told Ronnie
take his hands off her. And it cost Peter Rachman several grand

Left Underworld boss, Billy Hill, arriving back in Britain after being refused permission land in Australia, 1955. Bill really wa the top man – wha brains

Below The Messin brothers, Eugene ar Carmelo, 1956. Ju about every West End girl on the gam belonged to them and their brothers

ower sellers at Piccadilly Circus, 1925. This was the London I grew
 in

Rev. Harold Davidson, Rector of Stiffkey, with his daughter Patricia, outside court during his trial for grave immorality, 1932. He said he was saving young girls – more like, saving them for later

old mate, Jimmy Robson, the gamest of the game, with me,
arch 2001

e Hampton Court Palace pub, where Lennie Garrett fought with
mmy Robson

Left The Castle Hotel, formerly the Reform Club, Walworth Road

Below Marilyn with me and her parents Renee and Tommy Wisbey, at the launch of Marilyn's great book, *Gangster's Moll,* in what was Murray's Cabaret Club

exes out of it. We'd have about twenty machines there at any one time. They were always coming in for repairs – people would be giving them a kick or pulling the handle out of alignment and we'd have to have spare ones to take around the countryside. It was a tragedy about Atlantic; a good business. We never needed it to be hooky. When Eddie and me were nicked Leslie carried on as best he could, but then he tried to help us with a juror and he was nicked himself. It was really nothing. We heard that the brother of a juror went into a café down the East End and what we wanted was the truth to come out and get a proper verdict. The owner of the caff introduced the brother to Leslie and Billy Stayton, who used to play with us for Soho Rangers. The man said so far as he was concerned there was no problem and even though the police were all over his brother he'd mention it. After that it was all on top and poor Leslie got eighteen months. And that was the end of Atlantic.

2

Round the corner in Charlotte Street was that famous Italian restaurant, Bertorelli's, and we used to eat in there quite a lot. It's still there but I haven't been in it for years. I was in Chez Gerard though the other night, and that's nearly opposite. The Book Club ran a competition for people who bought their edition of *Mad Frank's Diary* and the prize was a dinner in the restaurant with me. You had to have a tie-breaking answer to the sentence 'I would like to have dinner with Mad Frank because . . .' And the girl that won it – real nice she was, her and her partner – wrote 'Frankly I'd be mad not to'. It was about the only time in my life I've ever been late for anything. I'd had to go and do a show up in the North. It was after the train crash at Hatfield and everything was running at quarter speed, so I was an hour late but she was lovely about it.

Charlotte Street used to be the home of the Scala Theatre which staged Maskelyne and Devant, a children's magic show every Christmas, and it was there in April 1947 that a famous robbery took place. Harry Jenkins from the Elephant, Christopher Geraghty and Terence Rolt did the job on a jeweller's which went all wrong. First of all the jeweller shut the safe door, then one of the employees threw a stool at them and when they went to get their car they found they was blocked in by a lorry. As I've said, in them days passers-by would have a go and one of them, an Alec de Antiquis, tried to block them with his motorcycle and he was shot. They was eventually bubbled by a man who'd been on a job with them in Queensway. Harry and Christopher was hanged, Rolt was detained at Her Majesty's Pleasure. De Antiquis was given a medal named after a man, Binney, who'd tried to stop a raid in the city and had been killed when he'd been dragged under a car. Funnily enough, Harry had been on that raid as well.

If people think that capital punishment stops crime then they'd better think again. Harry and Chris was hanged in December and when he heard about it on the radio a kid named Flossie Forsyth, who'd known them, went out to do a bank raid in Worthing. That went all wrong as well and he killed a guard. Then him and his girlfriend went off to Glasgow and he got caught when he told a taxi driver to keep the change from a ten bob note when the fare was only half a crown. His defence was that he thought he was being controlled by the spirit of that New York gangster 'Legs' Diamond, but the court wasn't wearing it and he got topped about six months after his mates.

3

At the top end of Tottenham Court Road on the left is Warren Street. It used to be full of used car dealers, who'd have cars in showrooms and parked on the pavement. There could be up to 50 cars and other people would just stand on the pavement and pass on the info that there was a car to sell. They was mostly for mug punters. People would come down from as far away as Scotland to buy a car. All polished and shiny with the clock turned back and the insides hanging out. Chaps wouldn't buy one, or if they did the dealer would make sure it was a straight-up one and the engine wasn't going to fall apart within a month. The dealers may have been small time and they may have been ruthless but they weren't that big mugs.

At the lower end of the street they might sell hooky cars, but not the ones who'd been there years. They were hooky in their own way but not that hooky. At the bottom end if you'd sawed the engine number off then they'd be game enough to give you a price; they'd do a trade with anyone but the ringing had to be really good. Remember, there was a premium on cars in them days. If you wanted a new car you had to put your name down on the dealer's list and you might have to wait months. It was no use you saying you wanted a green car either. If a red one came along you took it or if you didn't the next man in the queue would bite the dealer's arm off trying to get it. They was making so much dough they didn't have to take risks.

And if you bought a car and it fell to bits who was you going to complain to? There wasn't these Fair Trading officers and if there was they weren't as powerful as they are now, and there certainly wasn't all these television shows and articles in newspapers. Duncan Webb had his work cut out with vice, not old bangers. Well, in a way they was old bangers I suppose, but Webb's sort sold more papers.

Some of the dealers had Spotty and Billy Hill behind them. It wasn't that either of them had an interest in the cars, it was more that their names were kept buzzing and it was good for the dealers to be able to say that Billy or Spot was with them. And if a firm wanted a hooky motor then Bill could arrange it for them. Mind you there was some good men who worked the pitches there from time to time. Old Alfie Alpress and his son Danny Teale were a couple. Danny was a top-class getaway driver. He could almost have been a racing driver he was so good. He got put away by that grass Bertie Smalls at the end of the 1960s and wasn't out too many years before he got cancer. He was game to the last. At the time he really took ill he was on bail for taking a mechanical digger to a bank cash machine. Parking wardens and regulations by the Council did for Warren Street in the end.

One of the big dealers in Warren Street was Stanley Setty, him and his brother Max who went on to own the Blue Angel in Berkeley Street – very fashionable that little club was and absolutely straight. Poor old Stanley wasn't straight though.

And that was why he got done by Donald Hume. Now there's one of the few men who've served a life sentence for murder and gone on and done it again. In a way he was another who was lucky he wasn't topped the first time. Stanley's real name was Suleyman Seti and he come from Baghdad. He was a banker for the black market as well as dealing in cars. He'd put up money for a load and take a cut at the end but he wouldn't touch it himself. He was a bit of a pimp as well and he'd got a conviction for fraud, which is how when they came to it they identified him. The Pros said Stanley got stabbed and cut up in Donald's flat at 623 Finchley Road. What was right was that Donald, who was an expert flyer, hired a plane and dropped the bits of the body in parcels over the Essex Marshes back in October 1949. What he never reckoned on was the tides, or maybe he thought he was further out to sea than he was, but anyway the bits floated back. The coppers traced him through the plane he'd hired and he said he was just dropping the bits for a couple of men who really killed Stanley.

Donald had a good story about how he had agreed with two men, 'Mac' and Green, to pilot an aeroplane for them on a smuggling trip. They had called at his home with parcels containing what they said were 'hot' plates used for forging clothing coupons. He agreed, for a fee of £50, to fly them out to sea and drop them. After the first flight, on his return to Golders Green he found them, along with a third fellow called 'Boy', waiting outside his flat and he agreed to drop the third parcel for another £100.

He put this third parcel in the kitchen cupboard and on the way down heard a gurgling from the parcel. He thought it might be a body inside and, possibly, even that of Setty because there was talk the man was missing.

But there was a lot of evidence against Donald. Notes which Setty had drawn from the bank were traced to him. He had taken a carpet to be cleaned on the morning Setty died and Donald had had a knife sharpened locally just before the killing. What he was lucky with was that no one had heard the sound of a quarrel and there wasn't a single fingerprint of his in the flat. Nowadays I suppose there'd have been some DNA evidence, which would have done for Donald, but there was nothing like it then. They got that pathologist Francis Camps, who reckoned that half the neighbourhood would hear if someone was sawing bones. And that was enough for Donald to get a disagreement. Of course, they were easier then, when it had to be all twelve jurors.

The Pros was never keen on topping a man after a retrial so he got offered the chance of a plea to being an accessory after, which meant he couldn't swing. He used to tell me he'd never have taken it if he'd known he was going to get a twelve.

Whilst he was away his wife Cynthia, who'd been a hostess, went and married Duncan Webb. When he was close to Billy and we'd all meet in Peter Mario's restaurant in Gerrard Street – it's a Chinese, the Harbour City, nowadays, best dim sum in London – we used to tease Duncan that Donald was about to be released and would be coming after him. He used to get really scared. Anyway the moment Donald's out he goes to the *Sunday Pictorial* and tells them that it was him killed Stanley all along; a quarrel over money. Don was only out about a year when he goes over to Zurich and robs a bank there. A taxi driver tries to stop him and Donald shoots him dead. The court said that this time life for a man of his kind really did mean life. But it didn't. Eventually he come back to England to serve the rest of his sentence and he was released. That was when he did a bit of electrical work in the flat Marilyn and me had in Duncan Street in Islington. Then he died down in a wood in Gloucestershire. It was days before they found the body and they had to identify him through his teeth.

As for Duncan Webb, when it came to it he died just before Donald was released the first time. He'd been to Liberia on a story for the paper on smuggling out there and he picked up a virus from which he never recovered. He had a big funeral, of course. Bill went to it. He really was the biggest name in reporters of his time. The other journalists on the paper made sure Cynthia got a pension.

Another man who made his dough out of Warren Street was Charlie Mitchell. He was a good thief. He could turn his hand to anything and then he took up horse doping. Unfortunately he turned into a grass in the Kray trial. That was one of the things which took the stuffing out of them, not that they would let it show. There was Mitchell in the dock in Bow Street with them, and next minute he's out and in the witness box so to speak. Later he was badly done over down the Fulham Road and went to live in Spain, where, I'm glad to say, someone topped him.

4

Almost opposite Warren Street on the right was Maples, the furniture store Alfie Hinds done, and Bert Sparks the copper almost certainly fitted him up for it. Alfie used to drive us all barmy in Pentonville telling us how he was going to get out of it – and in the end in a way he did. He was bright, was Alfie. He'd got an IQ of over 150 and he ended up a head of that thing for brainy people, MENSA. He came from round the Elephant and his dad had a flogging over a bank robbery down in Portsmouth. His mother used to wear fur coats from the proceeds of his dad's robberies and it was no wonder Alfie Snr was nicked.

Alfie himself was a class safebreaker but he didn't have all that much luck and for a time he was in and out of Borstal. Then it looked like he was settling down and was working with his brother. When the Maples job went off in 1953 he had a small bungalow at Wraysbury on the Thames. Him and his mates blew the safe and lifted a lot of jewellery. It was another of those cases where he was meant to have had dust in his turn-ups which matched dust from the store and there was some verbals. In the end Alfie received a sentence of twelve years' preventive detention from Lord Goddard.

Alfie never gave up. He complained about the trial year in year out. When he was in the nick that was, because he was a good escaper. He reckoned he hadn't had a proper defence because he'd had a change of brief and, of course, he also reckoned he'd been fitted up.

The first time he got out was from Nottingham Prison in November 1955, using a hacksaw blade and a prison workshop key he'd copied from memory. He stayed out about nine months and that was when Patsy Fleming and me got him an interview with Duncan Webb. Of course the more he got his name in the papers the better people liked him and there was all sorts of people lined up to write about him including that 'Mad Parson' John Allen. Alfie got caught in Dublin in the July, and he did even better when he successfully defended himself on a charge of prison breaking.

The next time he got out was when he locked a screw in the khazi in the Law Courts, but it was more like nine hours this time not nine months. He got out again in 1958 and stayed away for two years. He was a hero. Once they picked him up all he would do was talk about how he was to go to the House of Lords. But when he got there that didn't do him no good either.

Finally, he got a turn up when the copper Herbert Sparks wrote an article saying that Alfie should grow up and take his punishment like a man, so Alfie sued him for libel. He was lucky. People could still remember the Challenor case, and they was beginning to realise that the coppers weren't always on the up. During the case Sparks didn't do well in the box and at one time covered his face and a wag called, 'Watch out! He's doing a Challenor'. Of course the judge was against Alfie but the jury gave him £1,300. Alfie wasn't satisfied. He was a free man to all intents and purposes, but he wanted to clear his name and so he went back to the Court of Appeal but they wasn't being fooled. I saw him from time to time after his release. He died in the Channel Islands. I think by then he was a rich man.

There's a story about Sparks and Billy. The day Sparks become the new Superintendent in 'C' Division there was an article in one of the papers about how Billy was the King of Soho. Sparks had Billy in. Coppers could just summons a man in then, not to charge him or anything, just to talk. Sparks yells at him, 'Hill, I'm the King of Soho, not you, interview finished.' All Billy says is, 'Bloody Hell.' But I know who ended up better off.

HOLBORN, CLERKENWELL AND THE CITY

1

Once you started going into the city from New Oxford Street, unless you peeled off into Covent Garden things started to get a bit shabby really, compared with Oxford Street itself. I had my first dinner suit from Moss Bros in Covent Garden. I suppose I was about nineteen at the time. I went in and tried on the various jackets and trousers and then when I knew what size I wanted I told Eva and one of her pals went in and nicked it for me.

Just off Covent Garden was Endell Street and in the 1930s there was a famous case over a club there. A cripple called Jack Neame and his partner William Reynolds got prossed over the Caravan Club. It was one of the usual sort of cases, men dancing with men and calling each other Josephine and Henrietta, but there were also women there. I still remember the newspaper report said that Neame told the court a solicitor came in and danced all by himself. It didn't help. He'd no form but he still got twenty months and Reynolds got a year. It may have been because of the blackmail of homos which was going on in the West End at the time. The coppers were still giving evidence about men dancing together and calling each other darling well into the 1960s.

But if you continue down New Oxford Street you come into High Holborn. That's changed beyond recognition. Down the bottom end there used to be a big department store, Gamages, but compared to say Selfridges that was a bit shabby and all. Not that Eva and her mates didn't get a very nice wage out of the place. It wasn't the first place they'd go, more if they'd had a bad day they could always do a bit of business on the way home.

Almost opposite Gamages used to be the *Daily Mirror* building in New Fetter Lane and that's where there was a payroll raid in June 1978 when a guard was shot and around £200,000 stolen. My boy Frank was said to have been on it, and another job the previous year at Williams & Glyn's Bank in the City, but it all worked out well. Some police went to see George Copley in his cell and offered him a deal that if he pleaded guilty and give evidence against some detectives who was being done for corruption he'd only get five years. George had a tape recorder hidden in a wad of depositions and when the Pros heard what George had recorded the case got dropped against both him and my boy.

The raid on Williams & Glyn's on 27 September 1977 was a smart one. My David was said to have been on that one. It was a Securicor job. Just after 11 a.m. the van arrived at the bank and the robbers struck. The driver was shot in the leg and they snatched just over half a million. They got into a Ford Transit but that got snarled up and then they got to another van and that too got stuck in the traffic. They'd left over half in the first van. There were three getaway cars but the trouble was the traffic. They made it to the third but by this time the alarm was up and another security vehicle rammed theirs. So they held up a Mercedes and got away in that. There was a couple hanging on to the doors trying to get in. Eventually they abandoned the Merc and took a taxi. The police was keen to write it up as a Bungling Gang, but they still got away with nearly a quarter of a million. Funnily enough, it was in Birchin Lane where Ralph Binney was killed in December 1944. He was dragged nearly a mile after he tried to stop a getaway car and they struck a medal for his gallantry.

2

A bit after the war there was a very famous murder, still unsolved, in High Holborn when Daisy Wallis, the woman who ran the Adelphi Secretarial Agency with offices on the top floor of 157, got stabbed to death one evening in August 1949.

Apparently she liked to be called Dorothy and she lived with her parents in London. She'd set up the agency with what she had saved from her earnings and all she had was a couple of second-hand typewriters, chairs and a filing cabinet. Two sisters who lived in the building heard her screams but did nothing about it. One of them said, 'We often hear screaming and shouting, and take no notice of it.' The other one said she thought she'd heard 'Murder' called out. She reckoned it was a fairly rough area and much of the noise could be attributed to the postmen in the Drury Lane sorting office nearby.

She was right in that. It wasn't far from Seven Dials, just off the Charing Cross Road. It's still there now, but that and Drury Lane was a real thieves' kitchen in the old days. Back in the eighteenth century there was some famous names like Jonathan Wild, who worked both sides of the fence, come out from around there. Then there was more modern Jimmy Lockett, a great safebreaker who worked a lot with Cammy Grizzard, the fence. And maybe the best of them all, Billy Hill's family come from there. Big warren of a place.

Dorothy had been stabbed repeatedly with a stiletto-like knife and she'd bled so much that, when a sample was required for the autopsy, that Doctor Camps, who was in so many big cases then, had difficulty in taking one. The only clue the police ever really had was that a man seen running away was dark haired and of Italian appearance. One witness described him as clean-shaven, fairly thick set with dark hair brushed straight back from his forehead.

Two witnesses said they had seen her on other occasions with a similar looking man, once in a restaurant in Piccadilly and the other in a pub in New Cavendish Street.

What she'd done was kept a series of diaries in shorthand and when they managed to translate one of them they found she'd cancelled an appointment for the night before. What the coppers did find out is that every day she locked her office for a 90 minute lunch break but they never could find where she went. You'd think it wouldn't be Brain of Britain to reckon she was seeing a bloke but they never found him. Her parents said she didn't have any men friends and only a handful of girlfriends either. There was fingerprints all over the office and all but one set of them were eliminated from the inquiry. It seems the owner of that remaining set did not have a criminal record – which shows that maybe there should be compulsory fingerprinting at birth, like they say.

There'd certainly been a man in the office because one of her clients had rung in about six and spoken to someone they said sounded well educated and who said she'd gone home for the night. Then there was a mysterious Polish man who came looking for work and at the same time offering bigger space in a better class building. He was never traced.

A month before her death her office had been burgled. Funnily, only the older of the typewriters was taken, with the thief disregarding a £20 new radio and a cash box. For a bit the coppers thought that this might have some significance, but eventually they said it hadn't. Eight years later, when the office block was being pulled down, some workmen found a sword hidden behind packing cases filled with rubbish on the second floor. The coppers re-opened the case but no arrests were ever made.

If you go into Lincoln's Inn Fields there's Sir John Soane's museum. It's a lovely place with things like

Hogarth's *Rake's Progress*. It's where poor Dennis Bergin was killed back at the beginning of February 1987. It was a ready-eye since the coppers were already in the building. A warning shot was fired but it ricocheted and hit him in the heart. You can see the bullet scar in the wall on the right as you go in. They've got it preserved under a bit of Perspex. His brother George and a whole lot more got done over it. George got a seven. The coppers say they was after one of the paintings to finance a drugs deal.

If you stand with your back to the museum, Lincoln's Inn where all the barristers work is on the left. That's where the fraudsman Kenneth De Courcey jumped out of a window. He'd got a seven at the Bailey, and when he was having his appeal heard in the Strand he got permission to go back to his lawyers' offices to look at some papers. He said there was other papers in the next room he had to look at and within seconds he was out the window and on his toes. That brief Manny Fryde, who defended the Twins, said if it had been his window Courcey had jumped out of, he'd have been in the nick himself by nightfall.

You can walk on into Carey Street where the bankruptcy court was and where both Jack Spot and Darby Sabini ended up. Then it's into Chancery Lane and Cursitor Street where Freddie Ford had a club. Mind you, Freddie Ford had clubs all over the place. He also had that one in Ham Yard, the New Avenue Club. On a Sunday he used to send his punters over to the Cursitor Club. When they got done in 1925 there was over 200 people on the premises, a lot of them in fancy or evening dress, so it wasn't just a mug's joint. Well, maybe it was a mug's joint but they was high-class mugs. He had that bent brief, the Irishman Edmund O'Connor, defend him. O'Connor was meant to have been very good in his day, but the gambling got to him and he ended up with a seven himself just before the war.

Freddie got some form when he was young; a five at the Bailey in around 1912 and steady form from then on. He got chucked on a manslaughter in 1924 and got a bit more bird when he went down for receiving in 1927. Later he was a good friend to Billy and found him a very decent spieler in Ham Yard again. It was Freddie who thought of buying up hotels around Kings Cross and making sure the brasses had suitcases when they took the punters in. That way the owners of the hotel had a good defence if anyone said they was allowing the place to be used for an immoral purpose. He died a very wealthy man. Argyle Square was the big place for toms round there.

Like the Premier Club, the Albion pub down at Ludgate Circus, just round the corner in Bridge Street, was where deals were struck. It's got a brand new name now. The owner and his wife were great friends with Alf White's son Harry. That was where two coppers fought over a tape recorder in 1980. One of them was wired up against the other who was suspected of being on the take. One was Detective Superintendent John Keane and the other Detective Inspector Bernard Gent, and the fight was started by Keane trying to snatch a tape recorder from Gent's pocket and within seconds they were both rolling round on the floor. The landlady leaned over and said if they didn't stop she'd call the coppers and they said they were the police. Gent had been taping a conversation about a £10,000 bribe for Keane doing what he could to get someone out of a big blagging in South London. It seems that Keane had telephoned Gent, who was the officer in the case, blind, asking 'if anything could be done'. It was as blatant as that. He got a three year sentence. I'm not sure he didn't go on and become a brief.

Blackfriars Bridge was where they found that Italian banker Robert Calvi hanging in May 1982. At first it was said to be suicide because he'd been found with his hand in the till. Later, though, it seems like he may have been hanged by the Mafia for just the same thing. There was all sorts of talk about the bridge being symbolic, with Black Friars having some connection with the Vatican. I don't know if that's right. What I do know is that when that Judge John Maude sentenced a couple of irons for plating each other under the bridge he told them not to do it again, but added that if they felt they really had to they must do it under some other bridge, as that was his favourite one.

3

If you go down Theobalds Road towards Little Italy, Jockey's Fields is on the right. It's a little mews just by the gardens of Lincoln's Inn and that's where Billy Hill did the second of his big raids. It was on 21 September 1954 and the load was gold bullion being unloaded for the KLM offices. It took all of twenty seconds and the haul was £45,000, which wasn't as much as Billy got for Eastcastle but it wasn't bad at all. No violence, just a straight snatch. Speed was what was wanted and that's what they had. The coppers knew Billy was behind it, of course, but they thought he was in the South of France and so they pulled in everybody else who was anybody. One of the great things to do if you know a job is going off, but you're not on it, is to make sure you've got an A1 alibi and the best of those was to go round to your local nick and report something stolen. Get the sergeant to record your visit and there you are. You can't do that too easily now because there aren't many local nicks. Anyway, that's what one of the chaps who was pulled in had done, said his dog was lost.

There was all sorts of raids to find the gold and there was all sorts of fanny put up too. Someone had the coppers down at Surrey Docks one Sunday because there was a wire the gold was going out through there, but all they got was overtime. In fact Billy hadn't been in the South of France, he'd been with Duncan Webb and that other writer Hannen Swaffer who was writing his story at the time. Then the coppers had another go at Surrey Docks, and finally they thought Billy might have it at a toy warehouse he had in Aldgate. They turned out all the dolls and, so Bill told me later, it seems when you shook them they all went M-a-m-m-m-y. Must have sounded like a whole lot of bleating sheep. Billy went there with his brief because he was dead afraid of being fitted up, he was. That's not to say the coppers who did the searching would do it, but as Billy said photos could get mislaid or mixed up with others. The coppers found what they thought was wood shavings and Billy had them photograph them with a ten shilling note in the picture placed so you could see the serial number clearly. Then he give the note to his brief.

In fact Bill had planned it all within a couple of weeks. What had happend was that a KLM plane had gone down near Shannon airport at the beginning of the month and he had had people watch the salvage operation and report to him where the stuff was taken. That was how he knew it had ended up in Jockey's Fields. After that it was just a question of getting hold of the driver. The next year the coppers did a couple of men: the driver who'd agreed to let his van go and another man who'd worked at KLM. But they never got the gold.

Along the Gray's Inn Road was where the first killing of a copper took place. It happened in August 1830 when the Met hadn't been founded five minutes. He was PC Long and he followed three men all the way along Doughty Street, where that famous brief Geoffrey Robertson's got his offices nowadays, and into Mecklenburgh Square. He went up to them and that was when they turned on him and stabbed him. There was another copper nearby and one of the men, William Sapwell, was caught and topped. Apparently there was a big whip for Long's wife and kids.

It's funny how quick the police became unpopular because a few years after that there was a riot in Coldbath Fields, which was just near Gray's Inn Road, when a PC Pulley got stabbed to death as the police tried to stop a protest march. No one was too sympathetic this time and the jury went and returned a verdict of justifiable homicide.

The Grays Club in the Gray's Inn Road was where I had my party and a whip when I come out after the 20 years and I got a good few bob from it. Whips aren't so common nowadays. People might give you a few quid but it's nothing like it was. No sort of formal do. Even when my David come out after eight when he got mixed up with that crooked copper there was no do for him.

It was in Red Lion Street that Harry Barham went for tea in a caff on the corner of Princeton Street the day he disappeared. Harry Barham was a good chap but a bit greedy. If I say he was greedy it's only because you can't be a successful businessman if you're not. Once, when it looked like I was going to come unstuck after I'd done a tobacconist's, Harry was the one I got hold of and he came straight down and took the gear off of me. I don't really know that much about his killing. I do know Harry was in some trouble with tax and looked like he was going to get a good bit of bird at the Old Bailey. He'd been told if he pulled up money to pay some of the tax he'd stand half a chance of staying out, so he went round Hatton Garden buying jewellery on tick and then selling it at a loss. A one man LF really. Apparently he'd done quite well and he'd got quite a bit on him when he went to the caff. That was more or less the last anyone see of him until he's found dead in the back of the car. And, of course, there's no cash to go with him.

People said it was Teddy Machin, who was out of West Ham and who'd been one of Jack Spot's men. But since he's dead you can put the blame on him for more or less anything. Like Jimmy Moody who helped carry me after I was shot in Mr Smith's Club. After he escaped from Brixton with Stan Thompson, who'd been with me on the Parkhurst Riot, Jimmy showed up dead years later and if you listened to people he must have murdered half of London whilst he was on the run.

You can work your way through a series of little streets from Red Lion Street to Southampton Row and the Russell Hotel. That's where Harry Roberts stayed the night with a bird after the coppers were shot in Shepherd's Bush and I got hustled out of the Scrubs in double time.

4

If you go down Theobalds Road towards the City, at the corner of Gray's Inn Road there's the pub, the Yorkshire Grey. That used to be the hangout for Darby Sabini and the Italians of the 1920s. There was a big shooting there when the Sabinis were fighting it out with the Brummagen Boys and Fred Gilbert's Camden Town Mob over who controlled the racecourses. That's where Little Italy starts and that was the Sabinis' stronghold. Opposite the Yorkshire Grey was the old Holborn Police Station. The building's still there and you can still see the lettering in the brickwork. It's not surprising the police was on hand when there was that ruckus and a number of people got lifted. People from Little Italy just about stormed the building when Albert got lifted over some sort of driving insurance offence back in the 40s. They was very hot over insurance in them days and I'm not sure that Albert didn't get a few weeks before it got quashed on appeal.

The Central Club in the Clerkenwell Road was *the* place. It was known as the Italian Club and it was an official working men's club. There was a little porter's lodge inside the front door, just as they have in West End clubs, and you had to be checked in. That was good, because as a result of having a man on the door no coppers ever got in. Sometimes they'd have a concert upstairs and I used to take Kathleen, the mother of my first three boys, there at the end of the war when we was courting.

Next door was the Griffin. That's still there. It was where Tommy Bennyworth, who was known as Monkey and was from the Elephant, was knocked out by Darby Sabini after he'd deliberately torn an Italian girl's dress. Remember, Darby had been handy with his fists all his life. He'd done a ranked middleweight when he was young but he just wouldn't train. When Monkey's broken jaw had mended he returned with some of the Elephant boys, but Sabini had got word and with the help of Italian lads he drove them out of Little Italy once and for all. That was really when Darby came to the fore, and after that he was the Godfather of the quarter.

Monkey was a bit of a plague to them over the years and there's stories he did some of their men in a club in Maiden Lane off the Strand. He ran for a long time, did Monkey. He got off cutting the fence, Moses Levy, in the Aldgate High Street along with my old friend Dodger Mullins, Johnny Jackson and another couple of people I never knew, in February 1925. They and three others was all nicked and they had the very good brief G. L. Hardy defend them. I used him later in his life, but he was over the hill by then. They got a week's lay down, but it was all squared up the next week because Moses couldn't recognise who did him and the case was slung.

At one time Monkey was in partnership as a bookmaker with Johnny Jackson in South London. He was still around when I was a teenager. I know in August 1935 he was involved in the beating of a pickpocket by the name of Flatman in the Waterloo Road.

Bert Marsh would never go in the Central. Nestor Montecolombo, the brother of the man who got killed in the fight with Bert at the Wandsworth dog track would use it and, out of respect, Bert never went in. I used it a lot.

Tommy Falco, who had himself slashed after Spot put all of us away and then said Spotty had done it, always used the Central. He was very good to me over the years I was in prison. He was in Wandsworth with me in 1943, he and Jimmy Essex used to look after me when I was on punishment diet. He'd come and see me, put a bit of money my way, always send cards at Christmas. It may not sound much sending a card at Christmas but there's many who didn't. He'd died by the time I come out from the twenty and I went round to Leather Lane where his wife had a stall to pay my respects and thank her.

The Fratellanza Club was just down the road in Great Bath Street – now Topham Street – and this too was where the Cortesi brothers shot Darby and Harryboy Sabini after they'd fallen out with them in the 1920s. A girl got herself in the way to protect them. She was said to be in love with Harryboy. The Cortesis picked up a good bit of bird over that but they weren't deported. It was the end of them anyhow. Some people say that Enrico Cortesi was really the smartest of the whole bunch and that included Darby.

The Duke of York at the corner of Vine Hill was known as the 11 o'clock house by us in South London. For some reason it was open half an hour later than other pubs and when we left Vic Rosari's place in the Walworth Road we'd pile into cars outside and come over to get the last twenty minutes and an extra drink. Of course, in those days there wasn't no traffic and you could be there in five minutes.

What there was down the bottom of Back Hill was another place, known to us as the Italian pub, the Coach and Horses. There was also the Roma Club in Eyre Hill Street. That was a nice place. It opened some time at the beginning of the 1950s. The thing that made the bottom of Back Hill so special was it was really a series of badly lit alleys and passageways which all ran into one another. Coppers didn't go there too often and if they did there was so many twists you could get away from them easy enough.

When I'd had the really bad run-in with the Carters and I was seriously looking for Johnny, I'd meet with the Raddis down there by the bridge in Warner Street which goes under Rosebery Avenue. There could be up to 40 of us and we'd have a couple of vans and a couple of cars. We'd go off in different directions, asking where they was. Eventually just after Christmas Albert Dimes and I caught up with them.

5

I think the only case when hanging was in force and two juries disagreed was in 1963 when the Pros offered no evidence against Robert Reed in what was called the Holy Lady of Clerkenwell murder.

The Pros said that Reed had robbed and battered an old lady, Annie Mary O'Donnell, to death in her rosary shop in Victoria Dwellings in the Clerkenwell Road, in the early evening in the middle of October 1962. Whoever done it probably got away with less than £5 because the old girl kept nearer £600 in a body belt and that was found on her. She'd been to Mass earlier that evening and had probably been done during the tolling of a church bell at about 7.50 p.m. which the Pros thought had muffled any noise she made.

Reed had been seen near the shop and there was an ID parade when he had been picked out by someone who had known him as a boy. The man said he had seen Reed outside the shop, mopping his face shortly before 8 p.m. There was also his fingerprints on a Catholic newspaper and on a piece of glazed paper in the shop. When questioned Reed said it was nothing to do with him and he told the coppers he had been off work because he'd injured his thumb.

The reason his prints were in the shop, he said, was that he'd been there a few days previous to buy a St Christopher medallion for the baby his seventeen-year-old wife was expecting. He said he'd got no need of money and that when the robbery took place he'd been home with his wife and mum and the rest of the family. Asked if he was short of money he said, 'Not by a long shot'. That wonderful brief Victor Durand defended him. Funnily he was in the nick with Harvey Holford, who was accused of shooting his wife in Brighton, and he give him a Catholic medal for luck. It must have done Harvey some good because he got slung on the murder and only four years for manslaughter.

There've been some good bullion raids down Clerkenwell over the years. One of the earlier ones was in 1936, when four men just drove up to the London North Eastern Depot in Aylesbury Street and drove off with gold dust and bullion worth getting on for £3,000. There had been another just a few years before that in October 1932, but the most interesting one was when a whole lot of gold, something like £700,000, went missing from Bowling Green Lane back in 1967. No one was ever caught but that Wembley speedway rider 'Split' Waterman went down for four years over receiving some of the gold and smuggling, which was big business then. Years later when Alfie Hind's friend, Tony Maffia, got killed the police found a bar of gold which could be traced back to the robbery, but then Tony didn't get the name the Magpie for nothing. He must have handled every sort of stolen jewellery and gold which ever came on the market.

There's rather a sad bit to that story. One of the ways to get gold out of the country was to smuggle it in women's corsets – there were no x-ray machines and things like that then. A fellow called Mickey Kenrick was one of those nicked at Victoria Station on his way to Dover and he picked up a few years. Whilst he was in the nick the Twins was arrested and he was charged over an LF he'd been running for them. He couldn't face any more bird and he topped himself in his cell. What a waste. When it came to it, by the time they'd weighed off the Twins and the others, the Pros decided not to go on against the LF men. He'd have been chucked.

It was in 1976 that my friend Battles Rossi, who hadn't been with me when I did Jack Spot but still got four years (Bob Warren got seven), got chucked over the murder of Beatrice Gold who ran a dress factory down in Clerkenwell. There were all sorts of stories about why she'd been done – including to silence her because it was thought she might be putting the black on some people over the porn business. Bert was seen handing over a parcel just off the Strand to the kid they convicted of the shooting and the Pros said it was the gun. Bert said he thought it was jewellery. I'm not sure if the kid isn't still in and trying to clear his name. There was a story that a solicitor had set the whole thing up, but there's always talk.

I still go over in July to the Italian festival in Clerkenwell with Battles. The festival's really lovely; parades and bands and they carry the church figures from St Peter's. All the churches them days seemed to have a school and St Peter's was where I went. My mother insisted we went to a Catholic school, and so that was where Eva and I used to go before there was room for us at St Patrick's just near where I was born. We'd set off every morning at eight to get there for lessons at nine. And remember I might have been over the river and back even before that to get the stale bread from Soho. Harryboy Sabini went to St Peter's as well, but that was a few years before me. Bert's been a bit unwell these last few years but we still go out and have a few drinks.

It's a shame to see the church all chained up against vandals but that's the way of things nowadays. The last time I was there was for the funeral service for Alfredo who stood bail for Albert Dimes in his Spot case. Never hesitated when he was asked. He had that caff at Islington Green for years. What a lovely man.

6

If you went right where the left split goes to Rosebery Avenue again on your right you'd come to Hatton Garden. That place speaks for itself really; always been the home of jewellery from the days before the First World War when the big fence Cammie Grizzard operated. That was where there was a big pearl robbery in 1913. It was called a robbery but really it was the interception of pearls on their way over from Paris. Grizzard, Jimmy Lockett and some others picked up a lot of bird over it.

Hatton Garden had everything – money, jewellers, diamonds, pearls and not too much security. Someone was always sticking up a big job. In fact you heard of them so often 'looks like it's belled up on the outside but it ain't' that you got frightened and didn't do them in the end. If you listened to people there wasn't an alarm that worked in the whole of the Garden. What you really needed was a good bellman, someone who'd disable the alarm, and they weren't all that easy to come by. I had a couple of little touches, well not so little really, of wholesale tom during the war. You could sell anything then. Get your hands on a lorryload of aspirin and people would be biting your arm off to get to it.

It just shows how quick things could get to the Garden. Within 24 hours of Prince Charles having some jewellery nicked, cufflinks and a tiepin had turned up there. Of course the fellow didn't know where they'd come from and when he learned he contacted Scotland Yard.

The dealers, a lot of them were Hassidic Jews, used to stand on the pavement rather like the car men did in Warren Street. They'd have the ordinary stuff in their pockets and a little rolled up piece of cloth on which they'd display stuff. If there was a special bit then they'd go into the offices. Their word was their bond with each other, but that didn't stop some of them dealing in stolen tom. Funnily, there wasn't a great number of street snatches. If there was a snatch it was because someone had been stuck up but generally they all looked out for one another. It was a community just like the Raddis up the road. And again funnily the Raddis weren't all that keen on going down Hatton Garden. If you were seen people thought you was up to no good and so generally we steered a bit clear. There was at least one Raddi who had a place there though, Silvio Mazzardo, who was known as Shonk. He was the one who went down for receiving some of the gold that Bert Marsh got out of Croydon Airport in 1934. Georgie Shillingford, who was my wife Doreen's uncle, had a place there as well and so did Matty Constantinou who eventually went down for a VAT fraud. He was an ill man by then though, and he got a suspended. George was a good judge of tom, really one of the best.

Before that, in the 1980s when bank robberies became a bit dangerous, there was a run on VAT frauds through the Garden. In a way it was just a version of the LF.

Nowadays the old Jewish dealers are going but there's a lot of Afro-Caribbean and Indian dealers because their people like gold.

A bit further along you get to Holborn Viaduct where a hotel called the Holborn Viaduct Hotel stood, and it was there back in September 1912 that a company director, called Edward Hopwood, decided to kill his girlfriend Florence Dudley, who was on the stage. It was the usual story. He was married and she was saying either he left his wife or she was calling it a day. She said she wasn't going to stay with him and she was going home on the last train to Essex. On the way to Fenchurch Street station he shot her and turned the gun on himself. He wasn't that lucky with his judge because he picked up Avory. Hopwood said he'd been drunk but there was no question of the judge recommending a reprieve. North of the river it was, so he was hanged at Pentonville.

It was in Fenchurch Street that the coppers had their famous raid on Austin Reed in September 1980, the year the Countryman Inquiry into the police was going on. The coppers got called to a break-in at the shop and whilst they were there helped themselves to clothes, suitcases, squash rackets, just about anything handy. One of them was a DI. It's always good to see a few coppers get a bit of bird. Makes up for the ones who should but don't.

7

After you come over Holborn Viaduct you get to the Old Bailey. I was there three times and totalled 22 years, but I got off the murder charge when Dickie Hart was shot in Mr Smith's Club in 1965.

If you was in custody, and I always was, it was an ordinary start to the day. You'd have your cell opened up about seven in the morning and you'd slop out. In no time you'd have your breakfast and then it was the cell door open and down to reception. I'd always have my own clothes throughout, but some people would wear prison clothing believing theirs was being looked after ready for their day in court. Very often you'd be disappointed and they'd have been slung about any old how. Some screws were dogs – they'd deliberately loosen a button or give a shirt a small tear when they knew you wanted to look your best, particularly in a famous case. It's silly how a thing like that could upset you but it did. Gave you a bad start to the day and then you didn't think carefully, it was always niggling. What would the jurors think seeing you with a button half off your jacket or whatever? What could your brief do? If you complained to him he might not take any notice and if he was a good one and he did, all that would happen is he'd get a letter eventually saying 'all care had been taken' . . . 'no evidence to show' . . . 'done our best, sir' . . . you know the routine. By keeping them myself, I could look after my clothes in a respectable way. How well you was looked after depended on your visitors. You could have clean underclothes every day if someone would bring them and the screws weren't saying they were too busy. And you could have a pint of beer or half a bottle of wine and all. That lasted until the 1980s, I think.

You'd leave from Brixton about half past eight because in them days traffic, though it could be bad, wasn't nothing like it is today. It would take about half an hour. Once I was done in the Mr Smith's affray and I'd been given five years, I was a convict and so I came on my own to the Torture Trial with a special escort, hooters and sirens going, part brainwashing the jury. Sometimes it would be in the evening papers or on telly. It was like you'd see in the papers 'Police ringed the dock when Francis Davidson Fraser appeared before magistrates today charged with causing grievous bodily harm with intent to cause grievous bodily harm'. All that show was to tell the beaks that you was a real danger who'd leap at their throats if you had half a chance and if it wasn't for the boys in blue keeping them safe. So when the Pros said they wanted you kept in custody the beaks would know what to do. I never noticed anything in the papers like 'Criminals ringed the dock when three policemen appeared charged with bribery and conspiracy to pervert the course of justice'.

Then once you was at the Bailey it was down into a little cell, no more than four foot wide with a bed and table concreted into the floor. You'd often have to share it and then you got taken down the passage to a cell which was a bit bigger for your brief to talk to you. If those interview rooms were occupied then they'd turf out the fellow who was in with you and your brief would come in the little four-footer. Mind you it was better than at some Magistrates' Courts like Marylebone, where if you was in custody you was all in a cage and the briefs was pushing each other to get to the bars to talk to their clients and you was pushing to get to your brief. And in those days it wasn't a question of your brief saying 'Can I have a remand to take instructions?' The beaks didn't care. In fairness, I don't suppose half of them knew the conditions in the cells. It was a question of getting on with the case so they could get to their clubs for a good lunch.

What you got for lunch at the Bailey depended on what your family could organise. There was a big café opposite and they'd deliver to the cells in time for lunch. You was entitled to that if you was on remand and sometimes, even though I was a serving prisoner, the screws would stand for it and I didn't have to have the filth that was on offer. You were at the most famous court in the land and the screws were proud to be along there. Although they wouldn't admit it there was some kudos for them, so I suppose by their standards they'd be reasonably pleasant.

As for visits, you might see your brief about a quarter to two. Your barrister could come down the steps through the dock in the court quite easy, but solicitors were made to go the long way round and sign in with the screw at the gate. They could use up twenty minutes easy just getting in and out.

After court was over you might or you might not get a visit as a remand prisoner. Years ago you was entitled to it, but later it was what the police said that mattered. Screws were looked down on by the coppers so they would do anything they could to assert their own authority. The police might say they'd like such and such a man they was trying to sweeten to have a visit but the screws might get in the way, and the other way around.

Visits would be over by about a quarter to five and that's when you'd leave if you was special, otherwise it was an hour later, and you'd generally be back at the nick by a quarter to seven. They'd have some grub for you whatever time you got back, but even if you was on the dot it wouldn't be hot. They didn't have things to keep food warm in reception in them days.

In my time I can't remember a successful escape from the Old Bailey. Not those in custody. There was said to be one years back at the beginning of the nineteenth century. Some well-to-do man was done for forgery and that was a swinging offence then. His family had his servant wrap up his face in a scarf so it looked like he'd got toothache and switch places with him on a visit. The man was out into Newgate Street and off to France before he was missed. No one ever said what happened to the servant but at least prison breaking wasn't a topping offence.

Some did try to escape and I remember hearing about how a couple had been standing by the prison van when they suddenly legged it, but they was handcuffed together and they never stood a chance. The screws just lowered the mesh fence and it was bread and water for a bit. People have been off though on the way to court and there was a pair I remember, I can't think of their names, who went to Hampstead Magistrates' Court once and the screw told them to wait by the van whilst he went and found someone to open the gate. Of course, they was on their toes but they was handcuffed together as well and they was heading up the High Street when they come to a Belisha beacon. 'Left' says one, 'Right' says the other, and they just spun round the thing and collided with each other. The screws didn't even have to break into a trot to collect them.

In fact there was another go in April this year. Security isn't what it was in my time because only a few weeks previous some man had got at a judge and blacked her eye before he was hauled off. This time a couple of fellows on trial for robbery got out of the dock in Court Four and had it on their toes. They didn't get far. One got collared in what they call a witness support room, whatever that is, near Court Two and the other only made it as far as outside Court Seven.

I heard there was a hostage taken down in the cells earlier this year. Nothing was in the papers but that's what I heard. You can never guarantee these stories, but maybe it was hushed up because there's been too much bad news over security there recently.

The Twins was once charged with conspiracy to murder a man at the Bailey, at least that's what the coppers said. The idea was that a Scots fellow, Paul Elvey, would carry a case in which there was a hypodermic syringe which he could work by pulling a ring near the handle. It was going to be a bit like that Bulgarian defector who got killed in the Strand when someone stabbed him with a poisoned umbrella. The Pros said the victim at the Bailey was going to be Jimmy Evans who'd given evidence against Jerry Callaghan, Freddie Foreman and Alfie Gerard when they'd all been acquitted over the death of Ginger Marks. Elvey had kept the suitcase in his garage, along with a crossbow which he was meant to use on George Caruana who'd had a run-in with my friend Bernie Silver. Well, that's what the Pros said anyway. The charges got slung at the committal proceedings.

8

If you turned left and crossed the Farringdon Road on your way to Islington you'd come to Turnmill Street which was where I was shot back in 1991 in a nightclub. Marilyn got ne to hospital that night but it didn't half shake her nerves up. That was when the *Independent* said I was dead and it was over a drugs deal. Neither was right but there's no question of suing with my reputation. I've tried before and what did I get? A farthing. Still, they were decent enough to publish my letter.

The Clerkenwell House of Correction is just round the corner. Tiny little prison it was. It's a museum nowadays. They have a literary festival in Clerkenwell each year and one year they used the prison for an event, with me, Bruce Reynolds and Norman Parker, who got life for murder and now's a good writer, all speaking.

When I was on the run from the Harry Rogers' troubles down in Brighton, and he said I was leaning on him, I was very hot for a bit. I used to get my dough every week from Bill and I'd go and send it down to my wife Doreen from the post office in Mount Pleasant. It used to be open 24 hours a day. That was in the days when there was three deliveries a day.

Bert Marsh had his betting shop almost opposite in Exmouth Market. There's a lovely little caff there, Ayla's. I was in there the other day, quite by chance. I'd never been before but they made such a nice fuss of me. Wouldn't let me pay for my coffee and one of the girls there had me sign a birthday card for her boyfriend. When I think back, a few years ago if I went in a place and didn't pay for my coffee the coppers would have called it protection. I suppose it's one good thing about getting old.

9

Walk left down the Farringdon Road and on down to Kings Cross and that brings you to where the Whites used to hang out after the war. One of their earners was taking money off street bookmakers. Bookmaking except on course was illegal then and there'd always be bookies' runners, very often newspaper sellers, who took bets. Big Alf White would run things from the Bell or from Hennekey's in the Pentonville Road. No swearing or vulgar talk. A warning and then out. He'd grown up with the Sabinis, but he didn't really like the Jewish element who ran with them because Darby really didn't have prejudices. When they sorted out the bookmaking pitches at the racecourses, and who would run them between the wars, Alf got himself made Chief Steward of the Racecourse Bookmakers' Protection Association. He was in and out of the nick for the Sabinis. He got convicted over the shooting of Fred Gilbert of the Camden Town Mob but that got chucked on appeal. Then he tried to organise things for Joe Sabini, who was doing three years, get him letters sent in and better food, but the screw went bent on him and he picked up eighteen months. I think the last time he went inside was in July 1935 when he got twelve months' hard labour for doing the licensee of the Yorkshire Stingo in the Marylebone Road.

Big strong man, Alf was, but maybe not firm enough because he allowed a team of young kids to do him at Harringay dog track before the war and he didn't take any prisoners afterwards.

Jock Wyatt was one of the big men on his team. Before that Jock had been with Billy Hill during the war, when they picked up a four apiece at the Old Bailey in the 1940s. He'd been on the White strength for years. In fact he was living with Margaret White in Swinton Street almost opposite the Magistrates' Court there. Robert Staggs lived in the same street. In April 1951 the three of them got caught up in a very big job, along with Henry John Bryan out of Packington Street at the Angel and a few others.

It was all over keys for post offices around the country and they was eventually pulled down in Hampshire. What the Pros said had happened was that George Allen out of

Mildmay Grove had been employed by a big safe firm and he'd made about twenty sets of keys, and the places the team was said to have done was all over London and the South. The Flying Squad had been watching them for some time and it was all on top when a couple of them was nicked in Waterlooville down in Hampshire. Jock did his best to row as many people out as possible but it was never going to be no good. He drew an eight. Funnily enough, the man who was meant to defend me on the Parkhurst Riot but couldn't because of the election, Billy Rees-Davies, was defending a couple of the people and Joe Moloney who did actually pros me was the Pros then. Although they couldn't exactly put it down to Jock and the others, they said that something like 200 post office safes had been done using spare keys and they'd been at it for years.

Eddie Raimo was another from Clerkenwell. He could have a good row and once he put a glass in Billy Hill's face so bad Bill had to have surgery. Eddie was first a Sabini and then a White man. He was as small as me and he did a bit of time with me in the glasshouse during the war. It was about that time he done some bird for slashing George Sewell, the father of the television actor. Eddie was in Wandsworth with me in 1943 when doing his time for Sewell. George Snr had fancied himself as a cobbles fighter and he wrote his memoirs about how he was known as the Cobblestone Kid and fought alongside Darby Sabini. Looking back, I'm not sure he was as great as all that. He was keen to dish it out but he wasn't all that keen to take it.

After the war, when there was a row between Spot and White over the point-to-point pitches, Harry White was hoping Eddie would do the business for him but he was getting old and he copped it himself. Spot did him at Yarmouth Races and that was really the beginning of the end of the Whites.

It was in early 1940 that me and Patsy Fleming did Bravington's, the big jeweller's in Kings Cross on the corner of the Pentonville Road. We got spotted coming out and there was a car chase which ended with Patsy escaping over a wall which had barbed wire on top and me getting caught up. At least he got some of the rings. I ended up losing my brief. I was disqualified from driving for ten years at Stamford House Juvenile Court. They used to hold the hearings in the remand centre itself, just so the magistrates would know what type of a kid you was before they even heard the evidence. What a savage sentence that was. I was just a kid and there hadn't even been a crash. I wasn't driving even. I was given a day's detention and fined a shilling as well.

After that I never bothered to get a licence. I think the first car I had was a Saab in the 1960s. One of the good things about not getting a brief was I could say I couldn't drive and I was banned so I didn't have the aggro of being the one who had to go out and nick a motor.

The Scots Boys ran Kings Cross for a time. That's where they got off the train from Glasgow and that's where they settled in during the 50s and 60s. Some were good thieves, some just copped a quid off the brasses. Andy Anderson was a Kings Cross man. He was the one who escaped quite by chance when Ronnie Biggs got over the wall at Wandsworth and made his way to Atlantic Machines. Later, he was in the Parkhurst Riot with us. When I turned down George Shindler as my QC because he'd prossed one of my boys, Andy had him and, good luck to him, he got an acquittal.

By the 1990s, though, it was a real dump. Most places round railway stations are bad but this was worse than awful. In just nine days in March 1993 seven people died from heroin overdoses within 250 yards of the station, mostly round Argyle Square. There was a big clean-up.

Dealers had been coming from all over – Naples and Sardinia as well as the usual suppliers – and the coppers eventually rounded up over 60 dealers.

I think the area's on its way up again now – gentrification, they call it.

NORTH LONDON

1

Every now and again I do a talk for Gary Mason, who used to be the editor of *Police Review*. It's funny how I'm helping anyone who had anything to do with the law, but he teaches kids journalism and I go down so they can interview me and write it up for one of their classes. We always meet at the Angel and walk down to the City University where he lectures. On the way we pass the Empress of Russia pub, it's a coffee bar now. That was where Ernie Isaacs had a bent screw who worked at Pentonville. It was the same as Jimmy Robson had in Parkhurst. You could get him to buy things for you – at a price of course – and the meets always took place in the pub there. I think the screw got promoted to principal later, which shows how clever he was.

Ernie's death in 1966 was a bit of a locked room mystery really. He was shot in the basement of his home in Penn Street, Hoxton. There's no doubt he was a frightened man because a bit before the shooting he'd been trying to get some ammunition for a Luger he kept in the glove compartment of his car. He went as usual to the pub, the Merry Monarch in Copley Street, and he must have been shot as soon as he got home. His wife found him when she went downstairs with the baby about five o'clock. There was a story doing the rounds that he was going to grass some people up and that was why he was done. His first conviction had been for stealing pincushions when he was eleven.

Another of the great escapes was by Teddie Rice and his mates out of Strangeways, the Manchester prison, in

November 1954. Teddie come from Whitmore Street in Shoreditch. He was a good man, little baby face, you wouldn't think twice to look at him, wore spectacles for a start, but he was a terror in his way. He'd got ten years PD (Preventative Detention) in March 1954 for conspiracy and wounding. Him and Tommy Greenwood, who had also come from round Shoreditch and moved up to Manchester, was the real leaders, along with a number of big names from there. Eddie had copped it after he had broken into a bookmaker's in Levershulme. He'd been a tobacco baron in the nick but he did well because he wasn't even fancied as an escaper.

Tommy was a great escaper. He'd got out of the Manchester Sessions back in 1945, when he and a few others just threw a coat over a screw as they went to the cells, nicked his keys and they was off. That one only lasted a day. Then after he got released in 1947 he got done for breaking and entering and this time he was over the wall at Strangeways, climbing through the prison workshop roof.

That's what they did in 1954. The workshop was very near the wall and the wall wasn't a big one. You might have thought that the screws would have learned something. They may have done but the authorities hadn't. In them days there was really very little security. Prisoners didn't escape because they didn't think it could be so easy. They was sure there was a trick somewhere and the moment they got out there'd be someone come out of a doorway. It's like them fake burglar alarms people have today. You know it's a moody, but you don't want to take the chance.

Anyway they sawed through a bar in the skylight of the mailbag shop and was on to the roof and away. The telly showed their pictures but that didn't do much good. They was old ones from their files at Scotland Yard and didn't look nothing like them.

What baffled the coppers was where they had gone. It was a fair bet that the Manchester fellows would have stayed up north and Tommy Greenwood might make for his mother's, but Eddie Rice was the one they really wanted. In fact what had happened was that Jimmy Robson and Danny Swain went up for him. Obviously if you're going to have a successful break you've got to have it arranged on the outside. It's no use getting over the wall and finding the only way out is on a tram. Jimmy and Danny was very good and they knew exactly what they was doing.

For nearly a week no one knew where they all was and as usual every break-in and nicking was put down to them. There was even some story that they'd been sprung so they could do a really big job. Then one of them did a funny thing. Tommy Greenwood wrote to Duncan Webb saying the reason they'd escaped was to show up the criminal justice system and that the only thing left for men with fourteen years' PD was to try to escape. He put a fingerprint on the letter to show it was genuine. That must be where the Twins got the idea from, when they had Frank Mitchell write letters after they'd sprung him from Dartmoor.

One by one the others got nicked. There's rather a sad story about one of them, George Davis. He hadn't been married long and his wife had left him. He heard there was a reward of £250 going for his arrest and he decided to turn himself in. If he went back home then she could claim the reward. So he goes and breaks into the place where she's living and hides in the attic, but some nosey neighbour sees him and calls the coppers. His poor wife – who never knew he was there – was lucky not to get done for harbouring and it was some other woman who picked up the dough.

The last ones to be found was Tommy Greenwood and Eddie Rice. The coppers got on to Tommy because there was a girl who'd been sent money to come down from Manchester and stay with him. They'd quarrelled and she'd left. She hadn't any money to get back home and so she went to the police. And that left Eddie.

It was only a matter of time before he was grassed up and it was another woman who did it. Now the coppers reckoned he was living in West End Lane, Kilburn, and they started staking out the place and the new milkman and the relief postman were coppers. That sort of caper. The trouble was that the man there didn't look much like Eddie.

They got him at the beginning of February, the day before he was going to hop it. When they did they found a load of tobacco and cash. They dug up the garden and found a load of jelly as well. He got thirteen years' PD at the Old Bailey, concurrent with the ten he was doing, but he never ever said how the escape was planned. I met him in the nick a number of times but when he come out he just sort of faded from the scene.

2

There have been some good people and families come out of Islington. Marilyn and me lived there for years in a little flat in Duncan Street just near the antique market. That wasn't far from where she had a drinker for a short time, before she got run off the patch by some of the other local talent and before she met me. Then there was the City Club not a couple of hundred yards away. That was owned by Georgie Bell at one time. He was a good man. He got shot by a junkie but I'm glad to say he survived.

I was away during the great days of the City Club but I heard all about it. I think it was there that David Knight took a beating from Johnny Isaacs, Ernie's brother, which ended up at the Old Bailey with David's brother, Ronnie Knight, charged with the murder of Tony Zomparelli. I'm pleased to say he was chucked. He was very good to me when I went over to Spain to collect some money on Charlie Richardson's behalf and got nicked at Malaga airport.

One of the other businesses Marilyn had in Islington was a sauna in Upper Street. When she first took me to see it I couldn't believe my eyes: it was in the same building as a tailor's shop I'd screwed in 1943. Everybody around the Angel got measured up in the place. You had half-day closing then and me and two others did it in the afternoon. One of the fellow's sisters was going with Albie Hoy who was a top man at the Angel and he put it up for us. We cleared the place of suits and cloth and had our hands bitten off by other tailors who wanted the stuff. Albie was another who got cut by Hoppy Smith but to his credit he went back and did him. He got a seven after the war, over a security van I think it was. He's long dead now.

3

One of the vice merchants of London after the Messinas was a man called Maurice Conley.[1] He was another who got exposed by Duncan Webb. He had a few clubs, including the Carousel and the Hollywood in Curzon Street, but he also had the Little Club in the Brompton Road. When I was on the run from South London I went and stayed over in Notting Hill and I got quite friendly with the mob there. They used to wander down for a drink in the Little Club and I'd go with them. The place was full of brasses they called hostesses but we wasn't there as punters. We'd say 'Hello, girls' to the brasses who'd be sitting in little cubicles, and they'd say 'Hello, boys' and if things was slack with them we'd send them over a drink

---

[1] In 1961 at Marylebone Magistrates' Court Conley admitted running a brothel at the Court Club and was fined £100 and ordered to pay 25 guineas costs.

sometimes. Ruth Ellis was one of the brasses. It was only when she was in the papers that one of the mob told me who she was. I'd never known her name, she was just someone to say hello to.

Hers was a really sad story. If ever there was a woman who had bad luck with men it was Ruth. She'd come down from Rhyl in Wales to make her fortune and she ended up by shooting a man, David Blakely, outside the Magdala pub in Hampstead. Rhyl was an unlucky town. It was there James Hanratty said he'd been on the night he was meant to have shot Michael Gregsten and Valerie Storie. That didn't do him any good at all. I see they've done a DNA and it's come up that after all these years it was him after all. I know the family is challenging it, saying the sample's been contaminated, but it don't look good for him.

Anyway back to Ruth Ellis. She got put in the club by a Canadian who sloped off back home and she had to bring up her little boy, André, and so she went and worked as a photographer's model in places like the Camera Club. That meant posing in her underwear or in the nude for men, half of whom didn't have film in their cameras and got their kicks by saying things like, 'Look as though you'd like to tread on us' and 'I'm a worm'. Then she worked in another place, the Court Club in Duke Street, which later became Carroll's Club. Next she went and married a dentist. She had another daughter by the marriage but it didn't last.

It was the sort of time after the war when them people from the RAF was being demobbed; all of them officers with blazers and moustaches and posh accents, but many of them weren't really gents. All of them had been famous pilots, at least that's what they said. They didn't really settle down either after all the excitement; they didn't want to go back to being clerks. It was as if they was still fighting the war. A lot of them lived in a sort of half-world with the likes of us. Bit of buying and selling cars and other things in pubs and clubs. The really good ones would tell you where a whole load of parachutes was stored and of course we knew who'd make silk underwear out of the 'chutes, or they'd stick up a warehouse which had Scotch and gin for the local officers' mess. Then eventually they faded away, they finally realised that the war was over and it was back to getting ink on their fingers. Funnily, it wasn't the same with people from the army.

Poor Ruth really did tart herself up. She took elocution lessons and had expensive clothes and handmade shoes but when it all come down to it she was still a brass. She did a bit of blue film work as well. Then she met this David Blakely and he treated her rotten. He was halfway well connected and there was certainly money about. The Little Club had top-class punters and she did well. Soon she became the manageress and she moved into the flat over the club and he moved in and all. But he was always two-timing her and giving her a hiding for good measure. He had her Monday to Friday and then it was home to Buckinghamshire and his fiancée. What did it was the announcement of his engagement in *The Times* and it wasn't to Ruth. She was in the club again as well and there was another go with the knitting needles. Then he went off to the motor car races at Le Mans and stayed away and by the time he come back, she was living with another geezer, Desmond Cusson his name was. He had a flat at Goodwood Court in Devonshire Street.

When Blakely did come back it was all hearts and flowers. He broke off his engagement but it didn't last. There was always other women and it was back to this Cusson and soon she was having it off with both. Eventually Blakely won and they set up together in a flat in Egerton Gardens. She was paying the bills and giving him money on the side and then she fell pregnant again. He started building a racing car.

It all came on top over the Easter in 1955. He left her in the flat and promised to call but he never did and she found out he was at some of his friends in Tanza Road, Hampstead. Good Friday she went round but they wouldn't let her in and by the Sunday she'd got hold of a gun and in the evening she went back to Hampstead, found he was in the Magdala pub in South Hill Park and, as he come out, she shot him. The trouble was, and this is what probably did for her, she shot a bystander as well. Didn't kill the woman but injured her. Next thing she did was say to the police that she intended to kill Blakely.

Of course the Pros put it all down to her. She was the one living with two men, she was the one who couldn't bear that Blakely was going off. Melford Stevenson, who put Ronnie and Reggie down, was the brief who defended her then and he didn't put up much of a show. Nowadays as a battered woman who'd just had an abortion she might even have got probation, but then she was a scarlet woman who was having it off with two men. They did call a psychiatrist but the judge said that even on her story there was no defence to murder. She never even bothered to appeal. People said she was just glad to get it over. She was topped; the last woman to hang. The night she swung there was a waxwork of her in Tussauds in Blackpool. The man who give her the gun was Cusson, of course. The story was that provided she wouldn't bubble him, he'd look after her little boy. The boy took an overdose and Cusson died in Australia years ago.

Funnily enough, Marilyn went on a programme about gangsters' molls they had on the television three or four years ago and Ruth Ellis' daughter, Georgie, was one of the other women on the show, but really she was never much around the faces. Georgie'd had an affair with both George Best and Richard Harris and she knew people like Charlie Wilson but she wasn't really one of the chaps, it's said.

Some families just have no luck. She and her aunt Muriel Jakubait, Ruth's sister, have been campaigning for years for the case to be reopened, and just when the Court of Appeal says it will hear it Georgie goes and gets cancer. Her aunt's not well either. Life don't seem fair sometimes.

Maybe one of the reasons they topped poor Ruth was because of another woman who did a murder in the same bit of Hampstead just a while before. Anyway, people say that may have played a part. She was an old Cypriot woman, Mrs Styllou Christofi, who was almost certainly a double murderer. She'd done a woman back in Cyprus; now she went and killed her daughter-in-law, Hella, in July 1954. She'd been living for about a year with her son and Hella in South Hill Park and it wasn't working out so they arranged she should go back home. That's when a neighbour out walking his dog saw Mrs Christofi trying to burn Hella's body, setting fire to newspaper in her back yard.

For once the prison doctors thought that she was insane, so she really must have been off her trolley, but she wouldn't let her brief run that defence. The jury recommended mercy and she was examined again. This time three doctors thought she was sane. It was a bit like Straffen. Back in the early 1950s, Straffen got done for killing a young girl in Bath. They found he was insane and put him in Broadmoor. Then one afternoon he escapes and another girl's killed. This time they put him in prison. So what it means is when he walked out of Broadmoor he was insane but by the time he killed the kid – if he did – a couple of hours later he was sane again. The old woman got topped at Holloway. One of the things that did for her was that in 1925 she'd been done for that murder back in Cyprus. They said she'd pushed a burning torch down her mother-in-law's throat whilst the woman had been held down by neighbours, but she had been acquitted. It's likely that's what prevented her reprieve and, when it came to it, it helped to do for Ruth.

Generally, they didn't like topping women. Partly it was the mess. They made them wear rubber knickers when they went on to the scaffold. That was because women always crapped themselves when they swung, as did men of course, although men had their trouser legs tied round their ankles. For some reason, the authorities thought it was more degrading in the case of women.

Hampstead Heath was a real Gobbler's Gulch in its day. All sorts of people having it off in the good weather – and the bad for that matter – but you could find some really funny things going on there. Like the time in July 1968 when the park keeper heard hammering and there was a Joseph Richard de Havilland being nailed to a twelve-foot cross. There was all sorts of stories about how it was a sex thing, but it seems de Havilland had told one of the men nailing him up that by being crucified he'd make the world a better place with no sin and no racial discrimination. When it come to it, though, they seem to have been doing it for the money with photographs going to the newspapers. One of the men got a twelve month but they never prossed de Havilland. Maybe they thought he'd suffered enough.

There was another very funny case on the Heath in the middle of December 1991. A woman walking her dog found Ghebre Luul Kassa, an Ethiopian refugee, hanging from a tree in West Heath. He had been bound with white washing-line rope and blindfolded with a red silk tie. They reckoned he had been killed close to where his body was found and he had then been hanged. His gold and black onyx ring with the letter 'K' was missing. He'd had a briefcase and that had been opened and the contents lay all around.

The police discovered that the previous day he had spent most of his time at a café his brother owned in

Cricklewood Broadway. He'd told his brother he'd got a job working as a chauffeur for a wealthy Arab family. He rang up a garage on the Finchley Road where this man's Mercedes was being repaired and then after he left the café around six p.m. he was never seen again.

Of course, people thought politics, but no one could prove that he was close to any refugee or dissident groups. There was some story he'd gone to the Heath to meet someone around ten p.m. and there was another that it was a mugging gone wrong, but it was a funny sort of mugging if that was the case.

It's not the same today but when I was in the nick after Mr Smith's you could almost count the number of black people you came across on one hand. One of them was a fellow called Kayode Orishagbemi. He'd done a young girl, Grace Fayodi, who was related to him in some way in July 1966, but I've never been sure he really meant to kill her. He said she was a witch and he was trying to exorcise her, but the Pros said he was a conman who was trying to shut up a witness to his frauds.

The girl was found trussed up like a chicken in Merton Rise not far from Swiss Cottage tube station. All her hair had gone and her thumb had been crushed. Orishagbemi said he'd tried to get her to disclose her secrets as a witch because he said she'd made his wife ill. In fairness his wife was in hospital, I think she'd got TB. Anyway he'd hang Grace on the door jamb every day when he went out to work and cut her down when he come back. Eventually she just give up and died. He said she'd been pushed downstairs by a ghost.

What the Pros said was that he was running a scam, pretending to be the secretary of the 'London Girls Modern College' in Plimsoll Road, Finsbury Park. They found letters saying he would be willing to pay the fares of Nigerian students to come over but there wasn't any such college. He got life. A few years earlier and he'd have been topped.

You don't get too many killings in a hospital except by the medicos (just joking) but there was one in the Royal Free Hospital in Hampstead and it was done in May 1992 by the girl the coppers say was the first woman hitman in this country, Rangimara Ngarimu. She took out Graeme Woodhatch, who was said to have swindled his partners of over £50,000. He was in hospital having his piles operated on so he wasn't exactly mobile. I don't know that I'd employ her. First off she couldn't find the ward he was on, then next day she goes back and does the business. She then caught the plane to New Zealand. Unfortunately a bit after she gets there she got religion and when the police went and saw her she told them everything and the men who'd hired her got life. She wanted to clear her conscience, she said. I don't know of a second hitwoman but I'm sure there'll be another.

4

My Uncle Andy, who'd enlisted in the First World War at the age of fourteen, took me to see Arsenal on Boxing Day 1928 along with my elder brother. I was on my uncle's shoulders and we was on the North Bank opposite the clock. I don't know now who we played or even if we won, but it was my team from then on. If he'd taken me to Accrington Stanley or Port Vale that would have been the team I'd have supported the rest of my life. I suppose, by all rights, really we should have gone to see Millwall.

It was in the Seven Sisters Road down the Holloway Road end, not all that far from the Arsenal, that Ronnie Marwood stabbed the copper, Raymond Summers, when he tried to stop a fight outside Eugene Grey's Dance Academy in December 1958. The Nash brothers were very good. They and the Twins arranged for him to stay out of sight for a bit but, when it was clear that the net was closing, rather than cause them any more trouble he give himself up.

Sometimes Eva and some of the other Forty Thieves would go out in the sticks – that's what they considered the Holloway Road to be. There was a nice little store there, Jones Brothers, which they used to visit. It's shut now, only closed down a few years ago but stuff from there featured in one of the biggest cases of the last century. It was a first in some ways. The first time anyone had been nicked through the use of the wireless telegraph. It was the American Harvey Hawley Crippen and his girlfriend, Ethel le Neve. He was done for poisoning his wife who was some sort of music hall actress when they lived in Hilldrop Crescent. She'd gone missing and some of her friends reported it to the police. When Inspector Dew came poking round Crippen got the wind up and him and Ethel went off to America. The copper followed after them when the captain of their boat telegraphed that he thought he'd got them on board. Meanwhile they'd found the wife in the cellar.

Where Jones Brothers comes in was that Crippen had done a bit of dismembering of the body and said it couldn't be her, because no one had been in the cellar since he bought the house. The brief who was prosecuting sent the policeman to Jones Brothers and they was able to show that the pyjamas the bit of the body had been wrapped in hadn't been on sale before Crippen bought the place. That was the end for him. Ethel le Neve simply disappeared for years and years, with people saying she'd gone to Australia and so on. It was one of those things they had in the papers back then, 'What Happened to X?' And then when Ethel was an old lady it turned out she'd been living in Lewisham for years. The house where they'd lived got turned into a block of flats years ago.

There were another couple of big murders in North London around that time. In 1912 Seddon poisoned his tenant for her money in Tollington Park. That was the case where he made a Masonic sign to the judge to try to get him not to sentence him, but although the judge started to cry he wasn't having it. Then there was George Smith, topped in 1915, who murdered his wives by drowning them in the bath. He did one of them in Waterloo Road off Highgate Hill. Seddon's place is still there but that Waterloo Road is gone.

If you go out further you come to Highgate and the woods and the cemetery. The gambler Brandon Hale was shot there back in January 1997. He'd been given around £100,000 to launder by some people. Now, a relatively easy and safe way to do that is to play red and black at the same time on the roulette wheel. You clean your money nicely and that way it only goes wrong if zero comes up too often. Instead what does he do but blows the whole packet. It seems he got a beating before he was shot as well.

I was reading the other day they're not going to allow plastic flowers in the cemetery no more. Not posh enough.

5

Joey Martin, who was in the nick with me over the years, came from round Tottenham but that bit of London never brought much luck for him. He was done in 1960 over shooting a girl he knew and he was hardly out when just before Christmas he goes on the Express Dairy raid not far from the Wood Green tube station in which a milkman is shot. He got a six for the first and life for the second. I knew him well over the years in the nick. He was in Durham when he and John McVicar and Wally Probyn tried to get out and only John managed it. I'm glad to say at long last Joey's out and about again. He did well over 30 years.

One of the best of the bank robbery teams of the 1970s was the one really run by Bertie Smalls who come from Hornsey. In a way they changed life in Britain. Before then everybody had to be paid in cash, and so every Friday morning there was a load of trucks being driven up to banks with people's wages inside. On top of that banks were friendly then; just a counter, no grilles, no bars, no nothing. And, just like I'd done a few years previous, Smalls and his team did the banks on a regular basis. It was partly a result of that that the law was changed so that people could be paid by cheque, and it was certainly Smalls and the others who forced the banks into putting up grilles and bullet-proof glass.

Robberies wasn't always really organised well in advance because someone might go in Tommy McCarthy's Log Cabin in Wardour Street and say, 'Anyone want to work tomorrow?' The next day they'd go in, get on the counter, fire a shot in the ceiling, take the cash after it had been delivered and off till the next weekend. They made fortunes. And then, who'd have thought it, Smalls turns out to be a wrong 'un and grasses up all his mates. I suppose you might have suspected he was a bit odd because in his early days he'd run a few women – which wasn't usual. There wasn't half some porridge handed out.

There were some good men went down as a result – Danny Alpress, Micky Salmon and Bruce Brown, who was the captain of his local golf club in Wembley. Another was Bobby King, who I see died only a bit ago and who was a great friend of Bobby Maynard. And then there was Philip Morris, who also got seventeen years for the shooting of a milkman during a Securicor raid down at Ewell in Surrey. He took all the blame for that one. There was one other curious man on the raids with Bertie and that was Donald Barrett. He rather puts the bubble in when Smalls and Bobby King got out over a bank robbery in Bournemouth.

Barrett put his hands up. Then later on he became a supergrass on his own account, did his short bit of bird and goes out on other jobs and turns supergrass a second time.

Sometimes grasses live out their lives happily – I hope they don't. I don't think Smalls had that much trouble and, like I say, people worked with Barrett even when he'd done it twice. There again, you've always got to be looking over your shoulder. Take that Peter McNeil who grassed up a whole lot of people. He'd been a drug dealer himself for years and he helped set a trap for a man from Detroit who ended up with eighteen years. Unfortunately for McNeil, his name come out at the trial and he said from then on he'd be a wanted man. That was back in November 1988. It wasn't until the 1990s that he was done down in Hampshire. Opened his front door and whack.

Mickey Greene was one of those big robbers at the beginning of the 1970s. He got nicked for the Ilford bank robbery and got an eighteen for it along with Ronnie Dark – no relation to the one who was later done by John Bindon down in Fulham. It was the one where Jimmy Saunders got nicked and Smalls give evidence to get him out of it. Over the years from time to time Mickey and me were in the same nick. I saw he'd been nicked at the beginning of February last year. The coppers had chased him all over Europe and America for that matter.

He'd done about half his eighteen when he come out from the Ilford robbery and he teamed up again with Ronnie Dark. They were amongst the first to realise how easy it was to make money buying gold coins, which didn't carry VAT, melting them down, selling them back and this time charging the bullion house the VAT. The coppers said they cleared six million in just a few months. A few of the team was nicked, but by then Mickey got over to Spain in the days when there was no extradition. The next thing there was a story that he had tried to get a ransom for a businessman who'd been kidnapped in Spain but, if he did, he was on his toes before they come for him. Then he started moving a bit of puff – well quite a big bit, actually – and he got caught for a couple of kilos. He got bail and was on his toes to Morocco but he had to leave behind all sorts of boats he owned.

Next he managed to get seventeen years in his absence in France – they can do that there – after the *flics* there found a whole load of bullion and cocaine, but no Mickey, in his flat in Paris. He was off to California where he rented Rod Stewart's flat under a moody name. The FBI picked him up whilst he was by the pool and put him on a plane. What does Mickey do? When it stops at Shannon he just walks off. That would be about 1994, but next year he accidentally runs over a taxi driver and he's prosecuted and banned. That's when people discovered who he was and he disappeared again. The Gardai took another load of his things, like his two houses there.

I was glad to read this summer Spain had refused to extradite him over here, but it still leaves France of course.

Islington can be a bit of a dangerous place. Billy Fisher, who was a friend of Marilyn's dad, Tommy Wisbey, was killed there in 1991. He just opened his front door and he was shot, and Brendan Carey was shot in the Prince of Wales in the Caledonian Road. A bit earlier in 1985 that moneylender, Alan Smith, who had a green Roller and looked a bit like Steptoe, was shot in the Duchess of Devonshire. He was having a drink one Saturday night in the pub when five men turned up. He was shot across the bar with a sawn-off shotgun and as he staggered out into the street he was shot in the head. He wasn't popular. If you owed him money he could be hard on you. They said that when people heard he'd been done there'd be parties on every council estate in London.

On the whole, though, you don't get too many professional hits out in North London but there was one in
Arden Road, Finchley, a couple of years ago when Saul
Nahome, who was said to be a financial adviser to the
Adams family, was shot outside his home. It was a job off
the back of a motorbike again. There was another one out
in Barnet; a fellow was shot when he come back to his
home in Moxon Street, just off the High Street, near a
trading estate. No one ever was done for either of the jobs
and I don't think they was even connected. That's the
trouble, you can rent a hitman nowadays for not much
more than a few hundred quid.

EAST END

1

I used to get all over the joint as a kid out thieving. You had to be shrewd enough not to stick locally. From the time I was eleven or twelve I was all over offices and shops. The City was the cream. Eva was that bit older and she would come out with me most of the time, sort of look after me. If I was caught – and thank God that wasn't too often – she'd be there to say she'd take me home and this was the first time and my Dad would give me a whipping, and it usually worked.

The East End was different; much harder work. Full of Jewish people, of course, and they were a bit warm in looking after their shops. Opportunities were definitely limited but what there was about we took and brought it back to the Elephant to sell, mostly through Lumps and Bumps, the old woman who wore no knickers and would hoist her skirt to warm her bum in front of the pub fire.

Funnily, although the East End was meant to be where the Chinese lived, I don't remember seeing many of them about. There weren't Chinese restaurants on every street like there are today. I suppose Eva and me just never really went into Limehouse which was the Chinese bit. We concentrated more on Mile End, round there. What people don't realise is that in them days the East End was a series of villages which was really separate from one another. People say the East End but Limehouse was far more different to, say, Upton Park than the Elephant was to Brixton.

Pennyfields was where the opium dens was when I was young. That and gambling clubs. It's where the man they called the Brilliant Chang operated. He was deported over drugs when I was about three but there was still legends about him. How he'd come back to England and was going to be like Fu Manchu and take over England. They was just old wives' stories, of course. There was a fair bit of smuggling Chinese into England when I was young and, of course, there is even more now. It's not that many years ago – 1995 I think it was – that a couple of Chinese turned up dead in Glasgow Road in Plaistow. They'd been stabbed to death a bit before, but it was only when the neighbours complained about the smell that anyone took any notice. The coppers said that it was to do with illegal immigrants.

I suppose Aldgate really marked the divide between the City and the East End. It's all changed today, but there was a tailor's the chaps used to go to just by Aldgate tube station. Max Cohen it was called and it had been there years – run by Hymie and Henry Cohen. I got my first made-to-measure suit in Brick Lane when their father had his shop there. Then they moved to opposite Sir John Cass School, whose emblem was a red feather. The story was that Cass had a haemorrhage just as he was signing the deeds of the school and bled all over the quill pen he was holding. I don't know if it's true but it's a good story.

If you stood at Aldgate tube station, looked east and turned left you went down Mitre Street. That was where there was a long firm running before we all got nicked over Mr Smith's. Long firms are nothing new, they've been around for years and years. There was about a hundred of them running at any one time in the 1920s in the City and Manchester. In an LF goods are bought on credit and sold and the vendor is given his dough. You do this a few times and build up credit and other vendors, and then you buy a whole lot of stuff on credit and knock it out cheap. Back in them days it was rare if anyone got nicked, let alone convicted. Firstly, you generally put in a front who had no convictions and you changed him around a few times, so that he could genuinely say he was only there part of the time. Then since most of the buying was done on the phone there was no question of identifying who'd bought the goods.

If the geezer was ever nicked he could put it down to inexperience and bad trading and, best of all, since both the coppers and the Board of Trade was involved they often didn't know what the other was doing and so nothing happened for months or even years. By that time the front man would be on a long cruise somewhere.

Another good thing about a long firm is that you can have a fire. You show the goods was bought and stored on the premises and it's gone up. Of course you've got the goods out before the blaze and so it's double profit. Then when the coppers or someone comes round you just say the business was ruined by the fire. Things is more difficult now but in them days they worked a treat.

This time the warehouse was to go up at a weekend but as luck would have it, after petrol had been poured all over the premises, the fellows who was doing the job saw a courting couple in the street. By the time they had gone the fumes had risen and so, when they aimed a Guy Fawkes rocket at a semi-basement window, instead of just getting a fire which would burn nicely the place blew up and demolished half the street. Charlie Richardson wasn't at all pleased.

2

It was round the corner from Mitre Street in Mitre Square that Jack the Ripper did one of his women. Well, around Aldgate was where he operated the whole time. There was terrible slums and tenements there; brasses were literally tuppenny uprights. There was over 200 lodging houses in Whitechapel alone, and they took in up to eight and a half thousand. A single bed cost fourpence and a double twice that.

The first of the girls was done on 31 August 1888, when Mary Ann Nichols was killed in Bucks Row, and the last was on 9 November, when Mary Jane Kelly was killed and he really took out her lights in Millers Court which was in Dorset Street. In between there was Annie Chapman on 8 September at Hanbury Street, and both Elizabeth 'Long Liz' Stride at Berner Street and Catherine Eddowes, who was the one in Mitre Square. He did the pair of them on 30 September.

There was a couple of other brasses done earlier that year. Emma Elizabeth Smith in Osborn Street on 3 April and, four days later, Martha Tabram in Grove Yard Building. Emma lived long enough to get to hospital where she copped peritonitis. There was a lot of fighting gangs and youths who went round demanding money so it may have been one of them, like the Old Nichol gang, that did for her. The other one may have been done by a soldier.

A copper called Ernest Thompson is thought to be the only person who may have seen Jack the Ripper, but that's if you count Frances Coles as being one of the girls. He'd only been on the force a bit over a month and he was out on night duty for the first time in his life in February 1891 when he walked through Chambers Street and saw a man come running out of Swallow Gardens towards the Royal Mint. He ran after him but fell over the body of Frances. It upset him quite a bit. Nowadays he'd have been able to have counselling and probably make a claim but there was no chance of that then. A James Saddler was nicked for her murder but the case got chucked early on.

In fact the copper did turn a bit odd and he reckoned he'd never die a natural death. He was right. He was stabbed to death at Alder Street and the junction with Commercial Road at the beginning of December 1900.

There was a man, Barnet Abrahams, accosting women at a coffee stall and when Thompson went to talk to him, he was stabbed in the neck. He held on and, so they say, died with his hands still on the man's collar. Abrahams claimed he had been given a severe beating by the police and so remembered nothing of the incident, just like Podola in Kensington all those years later. He was lucky with the judge because he got a manslaughter verdict and twenty years' penal servitude. It didn't do him no good, though. He might just as well have been topped because he died in prison.

Who was Jack the Ripper? Well there's almost as many theories as I've had Christmas dinners in the nick and none of them really stands up. It's almost as if people don't want him named because that would spoil all the fun and ruin the industry and all. The story I like best is that it was some Masonic plot or other, or that it was that James Maybrick, who was poisoned by his wife up in Liverpool, but who knows? I suppose if they could ever get DNA samples they might find out, but those who support another man would say the samples was contaminated and they shouldn't count.

One of the most elaborate murders down the East End in Victorian times was when Henry Wainwright did his mistress, Harriet Lane. It was a bit earlier, in 1874, and this time there's no doubt he did it. That was another of those cases where the murderer kept the body. He was already married, of course – a pillar of local society – but that didn't stop him and Harriet having a couple of kids. Then his business – he was a brushmaker – started to go wrong and Harriet was on the booze the whole time so he introduced her to his brother Thomas. She thought she was just being transferred to a new owner but they had it in mind to put her away. The day she went off, as she thought to live with the brother, she was never seen again.

Well, she was seen a year later because over the winter a paint room in a warehouse owned by Wainwright began to smell so bad that the tenants moved. The next summer he was made bankrupt and the warehouse was sold so he had to move Harriet. It's amazing what Wainwright's brother would do for him, because he agreed she could be put in the cellar of his shop.

They'd put the body in quicklime but it had worked the other way round from usual and the body was preserved, which was why it smelled. It was in parcels and Wainwright, instead of sending a boy for a cab, asked him to look after the parcels. Being inquisitive as kids are, the boy opened one and there was Harriet's hand. They put the parcels in a cab and Wainwright drove off to his brother's. On the way he saw another girlfriend and she got in the cab with him and Harriet. The stink must have been something rotten because he started smoking a cigar. Meanwhile the kid had found two policemen but all they did was laugh at him, and so he had to go looking for another pair. Coppers didn't go singly round the East End then, otherwise they'd have found themselves pushed down a manhole and been lucky if the cover wasn't put over them as well. Eventually they caught up with Wainwright and wanted to see what was in the parcels and that was the end of things. His brother received seven years as an accessory and the kid got £30. Wainwright got scragged.

3

I have to admit it, though I hate to do so, that Frederick Lawton, whose father tried to do me all those years ago, could defend properly. He defended in another East End murder towards the very end of the war, after Lilian Hartney was found early one morning at the beginning of August 1945 in Rich Street with her feet pointing to Grenada Street. Whoever done it had turned her dress back to show her fanny because she hadn't pants or stockings on. She'd been strangled and someone had bitten her. Whoever it was was missing a couple of teeth.

The Pros' case was that she had been done by her husband, Patrick, who had TB – which was a killer in them days. The story was that he was tired of her being out, putting it about in Chinatown night after night. As you know when people die, particularly when they're being strangled, they often have a riddle and there was a patch of urine in the bed. It was the same when Sidney Fox strangled his mother in that hotel in Eastbourne. The Pros said that showed Lilian had been killed at home. When the coppers come there was her husband fully dressed.

Though it hurts me I have to give Lawton credit. He hadn't much to go on but he got the jury to believe that this man who had consumption couldn't have carried his wife's body two hundred yards down the East India Dock Road. Wrong, when you have to do something, you find the strength from somewhere. It wouldn't have mattered much. Although he didn't know it, Hartney was a dying man already. They might have done him a favour by topping him, but there again they probably wouldn't have hanged him for what they called mercy. Just like the man they didn't hang, down in Hampshire, for shooting his wife because he'd shot himself in the jaw and it was now so brittle the noose was likely to break his jaw, slip over his head and make a fine mess of things.[1]

A bit after, a Patrick Hartney was lucky not to swing for a murder he done down the East End. The man was a regular burglar and he did for a Mrs Goodman in Stepney. The wire was that although she lived very poor she'd got

---

[1] This was the case of William Gray who ambushed his wife on 31 December 1948. He pleaded guilty to murder at Winchester Assizes and was sentenced to death but reprieved.

a lot of money. A neighbour called round one morning in January 1946 and there she was, dead on the floor wrapped in a blanket. The only thing that gave the coppers the alert was a bit of cloth on the pantry window. It was so small that it seemed like only a child could have got through but that copper Fred Narborough, who spent so much time trying to find out who killed a girl in Sussex and never managed to prove it, knew there was a dwarf in the neighbourhood. It shows how poor people was. When he got the pull he was still wearing the same trousers, which had a tear that matched the bit of cloth. His story was that she'd surprised him when he was screwing her drum and he'd thrown a blanket over her head to keep her quiet. He'd given her a push and she'd fell and banged her head. His appeal got turned down but the Home Secretary gave him a reprieve. Maybe it was because he was only nineteen or maybe it was because he was a dwarf.

Not that being a dwarf has always saved you from the rope. There was one up in Nelson in Lancashire, went and killed a woman in a burglary before the war. I'm sure that what did for him is that he went and hanged the woman's dog from the bedstead with a bit of string when it tried to defend her. He had not a hope in hell with a jury. Lawton's father didn't die when I hanged him and his dog on Wandsworth Common. Given the option I'd have swung for the dog, not for him.

4

Just about all the small halls have given up doing boxing shows. They used to be at the baths and there was Seymour Place, Manor Place near me, Lime Grove, though I think they did more wrestling, Porchester Hall down Paddington way, West Ham, there must have been up to a dozen of them. Now there's just about only York Hall left. That's just by Bethnal Green tube station. It was outside there that the boxing promoter Frank Warren was shot and the lightweight champion Terry Marsh got prossed. Frank, who's Bobby Warren's nephew, had done very well for Terry, but they'd had a falling out and the Pros said this was the reason for Terry doing the shooting. Frank had been on the way to a show when a man in a hood comes up and blasts at him. Not surprisingly, Frank can't recognise the man who's on his toes straight away. A few people chased after him but he got clear. Then a bit later Terry's nicked. He had that top brief Richard Ferguson, the Irishman, defend him and he got a not guilty.

Cinemas were thought of as easy knock-overs, and for some reason when there was a murder in one it became famous in its time. Maybe it was because real life had taken over from the fantasy people had been looking at. There was that famous one in Liverpool just after the war when Jimmy Kelly got topped. I see from the papers they're trying to re-open that one, prove him and the man who swung with him was not guilty. But the one I remember most was at the Eastern Palace Cinema in Bow Road in September 1934. The cleaner found the manager dying when she went to take some milk up to his flat. There'd clearly been a big fight and there was blood all over the place. He'd been hit on the head with an axe. Someone had opened the safe and a century had gone missing. That was headlines. It's not like today when a murder doesn't even make the news in brief because there are so many. A murder-robbery like that was news for months. When you think about it there probably wasn't 130 murders a year throughout Britain, and many of them was husband and wife and would get written down to manslaughter. It was really the same with robberies during the war. They made the headlines simply because they were so few.

The fellow that did the Bow cinema job, John Stockwell, worked at the place. He'd grown up in Salvation Army hostels until he'd been taken in by a lady in Empson Street. Then he'd started walking out with the woman's daughter, Violet. Good-looking girl she was from the photographs. Of course, the police started combing the neighbourhood but Stockwell had an alibi. He shared a room with Violet's brother and the boy said Stockwell had been in all night.

It's funny how when people have got money from something illegal they start tossing it around and everyone becomes suspicious. What does Stockwell do? He takes the day off work and goes to Southend. Then he takes Violet to the Tivoli cinema in the Strand. Long gone, that is. He's only just got work and suddenly he says he'll take the next day off and take Violet up to Lowestoft for the day. She tells him not to waste his money but by then the coppers know about his day off. She goes to work but he went up to Lowestoft anyway. Then it's just a matter of time. His picture is put in the papers and his landlady up on the coast recognises him. He sent a note to Violet saying he'd changed his name to Jack Barnard and another to the coppers saying he was going to drown himself.

Then he goes and leaves his clothes on the beach just like that MP John Stonehouse who was in the nick with me. It doesn't often fool people for too long. Fishermen usually know where a body will wash up and if it doesn't, well, then people start wondering. He went and booked in a third name into a place in Yarmouth and the manager blew the whistle. The police were waiting for him when he got back from buying new clothes. The jury recommended mercy because he was so young and he hadn't had any parental guidance after his father had been killed in the war, but it did him no good. His girlfriend visited him a couple of times. He had a pint of beer with his last supper and he's meant to have said 'Here's to the next world' but that can just be one of them things you hear in prison.

5

There have always been some dodgy doctors down the East End. The Twins had one straightened out and Christopher Swan was another one. He'd got a surgery in Queensbridge Road, Hackney. He took the place over from another doctor, John Peto, who'd copped it for not keeping proper records. The police claimed that Swan had been doing abortions and running a drug racket and he was charged with conspiracy. Eventually in January 1969 the abortion charges was dropped and he got fifteen years on the drugs, as well as soliciting a copper to commit murder. He'd wanted a few witnesses taken out and was trying to get a bargain price: four grand each for the first two, or ten grand for four.

It's funny how pubs change their names nowadays. In my time they never did but suddenly you look up and the Dog and Duck has got some funny name like the Fart in the Colander. There's two pubs down the East End, though, that will never change their names. Go down Mile End Road and just before you get to Whitechapel tube station there's the Grave Maurice. That was one of Ronnie's favourite hang-outs. It was at the trial that his brief, John Platts-Mills, started to explain how the place got its name. It seems he was some sort of Polish nobleman, the brother of Count Rupert, but the judge, Melford Stevenson, cut him off before he got very far so no one never learned, not that day anyway. The Grave Maurice was where I met Ronnie when he told me things was going wrong, and that the coppers were out looking into me and Charlie and Eddie.

Then if you go down the road just another hundred yards you come to the Blind Beggar, which I suppose is just about the most famous pub in all London. That's where Ronnie shot George Cornell the night after the Mr Smith's Club fight. That pub was named after a story about a blind beggar who had a beautiful daughter. Really he was a rich nobleman and he was disguising himself so people wouldn't marry her for his money. The other story is that the beggar was a soldier who got blinded in the Hundred Years War and his daughter, called Bessy, became a brass to keep him. That sounds more likely, and there's a Bessy Street off Roman Road.

George had been visiting my friend Jimmy Andrews, who worked with us at Atlantic Machines and who'd been shot himself, and he'd just gone into the Beggar's for a drink. It's funny how things come round in a circle. The record playing when Ronnie walked in that night was 'The Sun Ain't Gonna Shine Anymore' by the Walker Brothers and only this year they had me on telly explaining why that was such a big hit. Jimmy Andrews was often getting himself into bits of trouble. I shot both Checker and Teddy Berry over him. I shot them in the legs because I was only doing it to warn them. If you're going to kill you don't go for the leg. They'd given Jimmy a seeing-to and that was the comeback. Guns was easy to get hold of in them days, just as easy as it is now. The Malts in Soho always had them. Afterwards you gave them back, or if things had gone a bit wrong you chucked them.

Another very famous place in its heyday was Charlie Brown's. Really it was called the Railway Tavern and it was just in the West India Dock Road in Limehouse. Before the war people used to drive down there after a night out in the West End just to slum. It was an adventure for them, something they could tell their friends the next day. 'Oh listen, we was in the East End last night and look we survived'. The original Charlie Brown had a big collection of stuff he'd bought off sailors when they docked and he'd got some more stuff he'd show the men in the party in the back room.

There was a killing there during the war. A local man, George Gilbey from Bethnal Green, was done by a United

States serving man, Gunner Matthew Smith, who was only nineteen. According to the man who'd taken over, the Americans were 'blowing their heads off' by which he meant they was having a sing-song, and he ordered them out calling 'bring me my stick'. When he had cleared the pub a door panel was smashed in and Gilbey was stabbed. The boy maintained that although he had been there it was not his knife which had killed Gilbey. The really funny thing was they held the court martial in Regent Street of all places and he was found guilty and sentenced to death, but because of his age it was commuted to life imprisonment.

The pub's still there but it's changed a lot. The other big place, the Blue Posts, was opposite the Railway. Then there was the Crown and Anchor which Queenie Watts ran in Pennyfields, Chinatown. She was a great pal of the Twins. She used to sing the old Cockney songs for them when they had the Double R and the Kentucky.

Just like Soho, the East End was full of clubs and spielers and when it come to it the Twins was getting a good nip out of a lot of them. It may not have sounded much but it added up. The owner of Dodgers in Brick Lane paid them £15 a week and there was another of the same from a betting shop there. There was a spieler in the Commercial Road that paid the same as well. The Green Dragon in Aldgate paid up £40 and there was more when a blackjack table went in the club. There was a tenner from another place in the Whitechapel Road. And that was only a part of it. When you think that about that time you could buy a house in Tottenham for £500 you can see it was good money. We had one or two machines over the East End but we wasn't really interested.

6

'Little Legs' Brian Clifford was a mover, a buyer of gear. He did Johnny Mangan down the East End in 1979. Two in the nut and somehow Johnny survived and Clifford got acquitted of attempted murder. A few years later Clifford got done himself but there was no mistake this time. I've heard it said that everyone but him on his manor knew it was on top. People come to his door one night, pushed his wife aside when she opened it, thundered up the stairs and shot him whilst he was in bed.

People talk about gangland feuds but so much of it is personal and not business. It's never really been like Chicago, where Capone was wiping out the opposition to his booze trade. It was in Cheshire Street that Ginger Marks was meant to have been shot just after New Year 1965. He'd been out doing a bit of work when he thought someone called his name. He looked up and he was shot for his trouble. That was a mistake by all accounts. The man who was wanted was Jimmy Evans. At least that's what he said when he give evidence ten years later at the Bailey against Alfie Gerard, Freddie Foreman and Jerry Callaghan. The case was slung. That was another personal matter.

Of course so much of the East End went in the war. Places like Grenade Street where Zoe Progl was born just don't exist any more. She was a very good thief, hoister, screwer, anything really. She was a girlfriend of Tommy Smithson before he took up with Fay Richardson. She got out of Holloway, which was a pretty good feat, not too many women have managed that. Shirley Pitts, from that good family off the Lambeth Walk, did it too and she was well pregnant at the time and all.

There again you find places still standing like Batty Street near Brick Lane where the Jewish man, Israel Lipski, was hanged for the murder of one of the other tenants back at the end of the nineteenth century. He was found half-unconscious underneath her bed. The Pros said he'd been trying to rape her although she was well in the club at the time. Right at the end Lipski said he'd killed her in a robbery, but there's always been an argument that maybe he was asked to confess because there was such anti-Jewish feeling at the time and this was a compromise.

People have always said the East End is clannish and I don't suppose there's a much better example than when in July 1992 Kevin Fox, wearing a hood, was shot with his own gun after he had blasted the landlord's son, Mark 'Chalkie' Smith, three times in the stomach at the Memory Lane public house in Plaistow. The landlord had said he wasn't having drug dealing in the place. Fox had a gun and he fired shots at the crowd as it went for him. He was hit over the head with a fire extinguisher, punched, kicked and then shot. Eleven people were questioned over the killing but the coppers got nowhere. Good riddance you might say.

There was a couple of killings down Stratford Broadway which never got solved back in the summer of 1986. Peter Morris, who'd been about, was done a week or so after Micky Collins who'd owned the Moonlight pub in the Broadway went down. Micky had been a bit unlucky. Someone had decided to stripe him on the buttocks – noughts and crosses it's called – and they hit an artery. The pub he'd owned had once been in the hands of Bobby Moore the footballer, and Collins had been mouthing off about how he was going to take over the East End. That was one week and the next Morris is shot and stabbed outside the Telegraph pub only a few hundred yards from where Collins had copped it. No one was charged for either of them.

Another man who went down in a pub was my old friend Jimmy Moody, who helped carry me out of Mr Smith's when I was shot by Dickie Hart. He was killed in the Royal Hotel, Victoria Park, which was an area I'd had a wonderful touch in years before. On 1 June 1993 Jimmy was standing at the bar when a fellow comes in, puts two in him and he's off on a motor cycle. Jimmy had been another man in a good escape. He'd been in the Thursday Gang of the 1970s who'd specialised in blaggings and eventually when he'd got nicked he had gone to Brixton. Along with Stan Thompson who'd been in the Parkhurst Riot with me, and an IRA man called Gerard Tuite, they cut through the brickwork and were away in December 1980 and he'd more or less never been heard of again until right at the end. Then he'd been involved in a row with a family down Walworth way and had come over to the East End for a bit and he was living under the name Mick. I knew it was on top and that night I made sure I was on my way north, as there was nothing I could have done about it. After he was done there was all sorts of stories about the number of contracts he'd carried out. Who can tell? Maybe it's like Teddy Machin after he was done in a domestic in West Ham. Or that Gilbert Wynter who, now he's dead, is said to have done all sorts of things over in North London. As for Stan and the escape it was a bit of a waste of time. I'm glad to say the jury chucked his case out whilst he was still on his toes.

7

Just like Epping Forest, the marshes over Hackney have always been a good place to find things, and back in December 1980 the body of Colin Osborne, who was known as the Duke, turned up there. I never really knew him on the outside but he'd been a friend of the Twins over the years. He was a sort of minor villain really; a bit of a gofer for them. He wore a rug and thought people didn't notice. He got involved with Lennie Watkins who was known as Silly Eddie because, when he'd become rich from smuggling drugs, he used to light cigars with £20 notes. Nothing like drawing attention to yourself. Dukey, who was bright, was actually the one who put together this smuggling but it all came on top when a Customs officer was killed not far from Tower Bridge a couple of months earlier. I think there was a lot of people looking for the Duke and they wasn't only people from Customs and Excise. He was said to have had a heart attack but there was some story he'd been kept in a refrigerator – which I suppose might be enough to give anyone a heart attack. Watkins got life for the Customs officer and, after a breakout failed, he went and topped himself in the nick.

Rotherhithe tunnel was where I got nicked and pulled twenty months just after the war. Spindles Jackson, who got a two, and Charlie Rainsford, who got eighteen months, was with me and so was Danny Swain and Dido Frett. They got away after we had done the town hall at Rainham for some petrol coupons. We'd set off an alarm and we were chased all the way from Barking until we run out of petrol in the tunnel. I should have got away as well, but I ran straight out the end of the tunnel where the coppers were waiting, instead of going up the stairs which was an escape route if there was a fire. On the whole tunnels is good places for jobs. Charlie Knight, who was a top class thief, was probably the one who made the best use of tunnels. I remember looking at the tunnel from Waterloo Bridge into Kingsway with Jerry Callaghan just after it opened, and we was saying how if a security van went down you could just block it from the front and cut off the rest of the traffic with a Road Closed sign. We watched it for a long time but it turned out to be no good. People don't realise the planning which goes into jobs and half the time they come to nothing for one reason or another.

Nowadays the East End's changed. I was walking round there the other day in Brick Lane, Banglatown it's called, and it's wall to wall restaurants. Not like when I was on

the run from Stamford House and Patsy Fleming's people
hid me out down there back in the 1930s. The places just
line up one beside the other and I don't understand how
they make any money. There's also a lot of Yardie-like
killings down there. I was reading the other day that there's
more murders in the Lower Clapton Road than there is on
any other street in Britain. Where we used to have a
straightener and sometimes knives got used, now it's guns
and more guns.

There was a real spate of killings that year, in particular
all over London and the people who got the blame this
time were Yardies. What you have to be wary of is the way
the media hypes things up. It sells papers and it's often like
it was with Billy or the Twins and others like them. They'll
make out they're Yardies so as to get more attention and
some kudos. Mind you if you're looking down a sawn-off
shotgun I don't suppose you care whether it's a Yardie
holding it or someone else.

Things have changed down in Hackney from the Twins'
time and one of them is the Regency Club. That was really
their flagship, a nice place where you could take your
family of an evening for a night out, a Chinese meal and a
spot of gambling if you wanted. They once turned Jack
'The Hat' McVitie away because he was wearing Bermuda
shorts. He was also carrying a machete at the time. That's
where he was collected before the party in Evering Road
where Reggie stabbed him. It's become Trenz nowadays
and a lot of Stoke Newington is Yardie country now. Two
brothers and Leon Meshack Walsh was shot outside the
club back in April 1997. The coppers said they wanted to
interview a Rudi King but he was shot over in Walm Lane,
Willesden that November.

I don't care what is said, since that Lawrence case the
police have been treading very warily in arresting black
guys. They'll only do it now if it's cast iron. What is it that

Macpherson said? Racist conduct is racist conduct if that's what the guy who's on the receiving end thinks it is. Easy to put up, isn't it? If you're nicked and there's nothing found on you then all you've got to do is scream that the reason you were nicked is because you're black. You're the one who sees it's racist and therefore it is. Now black villains is poncing it for all they're worth and you can't blame them. I suspect there'll come a time when white guys will be able to scream they're being picked on and that's racist too.

WEST LONDON

1

What really was the best prison escape? I've often thought about it since the last book and whilst I've been writing this one. Sometimes I decide one and then the next day I think, no maybe that one was better. Was there one better than when the Welshman, Ray Jones, the cat burglar, broke both his legs getting out of Pentonville and still got away? I never knew whether it was him or Peter Scott who stole Sophia Loren's jewels all those years ago at the Edgwarebury Country Club out in Hertfordshire. May 1960 it was, when she was filming *The Millionairess* with Peter Sellers. Both Peter and Ray claimed the credit and it was a good job whichever done it.

I suppose Jones' escape could get the vote for the best of the single-handed escapes – no help from outside – but I think Biggs and Flowers out of Wandsworth must be one of the best team efforts. Talking of Ronnie, it's sad the condition he'd got himself into. I don't blame him coming back, doing it for his boy really, but I think if it had been me I'd have stayed out there, only because of the effort other people put in to getting me out and to Australia and then to Brazil. It would feel to me as though I'd slung it all back at them. I do understand his reasons but I couldn't have done it. I hope they'll let him out. If they want a hostage sort of thing I'd do a few years for him. It may sound daft but I would.

The time when the Twins got Frank Mitchell out of Dartmoor can't really count because he was on an outside working party. Mind you, Charlie Wilson out of Winson Green can't have been far behind the Biggs escape. People come over the wall at night, up into the security wing and out again. That was some feat and there's no way you could do that now. In fairness, when you look back it was incredible how they kept any men in during those days. What happened? The orderly officer went round early in the evening and double-locked the prison doors and then came and opened them in the morning. That was just about all, except for those walls with leg-breakers on them and a bit of wire.

But maybe the springing of George Blake out of the Scrubs was the best. After all he was doing 42 years for spying and you'd think the authorities would take extra care of someone like him. From the time he was weighed off in July 1961 there had been all sorts of stories floating around about how he'd tried to escape or how someone was going to try to get him out. You can never tell how good these kinds of stories are. There's always some con who wants to cause trouble to another or brown-nose a screw, and an easy way is to say that Frank Fraser or someone like me is going to be sprung. Then it's out of circulation for the poor devil.

There was one really good story about the Blake escape which seemed so far-fetched it couldn't be true. An ex-con who knew the prison well was going to be got over the wall into the nick wearing prison clothing and the trusty's blue armband. He was then going to get into the mail bag shop where George was working and take him out on some excuse or other. Then a helicopter was going to land in the yard, pick them both up and off it was to East Germany. The ex-prisoner was a sort of ne'er-do-well from Eton and Oxford – he'd been thrown out of both of them. The man who was to be the pilot was going to escape first and he was the one who blew the story to the screws. In fact the authorities took it seriously and interviewed everyone in sight and decided that the man who put the story up was mentally unstable. Fantastic though it might seem they couldn't rule out that something like this might not happen. If you think about it, well it could. People had got into Winson Green and got Charlie Wilson out. Years later there was a helicopter landing when John Kendall and Sidney Draper, who'd been done with my friend, Billy Murray's boy up in Scotland, got out of Leicester. There was one only the other day from a French prison.

Then they couldn't rule out an East German connection. After all there was Paddy Meehan, doing an eight, who got out of Nottingham with a load of others whilst they was watching a cricket match and came down to London where he got a bit of help from Eva before he pushed off to East Germany. You'd have thought someone would have heard bells but they still left George in the Scrubs. The place was thought to be just about escape-proof. No one had got out of 'D' Hall, which is where they had George, for six years or more. And they can't have thought George was much of an escape risk anyway, because they took him off the escape list within a few months of his sentence.

It all went wrong for the authorities twice over. Firstly, in June six men got out at slopping out time and five of them got over the wall with a rope they'd made in mattress manufacture from the prison workshops, and grappling irons they'd made from metal rails on the landings and stairs. If you think about it that must have been one of the best and all. What was even better in a way was that, although someone had grassed them and the police told the screws, they still got out. They'd even named two of the men. One of the men who got out was Martin O'Day, who'd worked for Eddie and me at Atlantic emptying the machines. They wasn't out long. Like I've said, that's the problem with escapes. It's not necessarily the getting out that's difficult. It's the staying out.

Of course, after Martin and the others' escape there was a great fuss with emergency towers being put up in

Wakefield and Maidstone and an observation tower at the Scrubs with walkie-talkies for the screws.

Then came the killing of the coppers in Braybrook Street, which of course was nothing to do with security at the prison except they thought, quite wrongly as it happened, that there was a plan to spring me. What had happened was that Harry Roberts, John Duddy and John Witney had been going to do a rent collector when they were pulled by some coppers over a tax disc. Witney called out to Harry to shoot them and he killed two straight off. The third one tried to drive away but Harry shot him as well. Someone had seen their motor and it got traced back to Witney, who grassed up the others in short order.

As I say, it was in the papers they had been there to spring me, and I was taken out of the Scrubs faster than you could say Old Bailey. Duddy's father had been in the Glasgow police; done years in the force there. I knew Duddy in the nick. He was a good man but you always look twice at people who've got relatives in the police. That other one, Witney, he not only grassed them up, he grassed people up in the nick and all. Who would have visualised he was a right snide? When Charlie Richardson and the others did that great feat in Durham and barricaded themselves in the prison officers' room and were going through the papers, Witney was meant to be with them but he went and locked himself in his cell like the coward he was.

Duddy died in the nick and Witney was released some years ago. Then in 1999 there was a good piece of news in the papers for once. Someone had killed him in Bristol where he was living. I'm not sure the whole story come out in court but a much younger fellow, Nigel Evans, went and hit him with a meat tenderiser after a quarrel over the rent. He said he'd only done it when Witney attacked first but the jury was against him. Evans also went and pleaded guilty to stealing Witney's cheque book and bank card and he got life in May last year. Harry is in an open prison and with luck by the time this book comes out he may have been released. I knew him well in the nick. His mother, who used to visit him all round the country, was a lovely woman.

But, back in 1965, they still didn't move George Blake. Really, when you think of it they'd only themselves to blame when he walked out – which is what he did on 22 October that year. The cons had been watching the wrestling on ITV and he was telling a couple of screws at 5.30 p.m. how he thought it had been faked and by half six at the very latest, some people say it was by six, he was gone. He'd gone onto the landing on the second floor and kicked the bars of the window. There was then a drop of a bit over twenty feet but he could get onto a covered way which was about half the distance and then, if he lowered himself off, it was a drop of no more than four feet. It was raining at the time and the visibility was poor and he'd only got twenty yards to cover to the prison wall. He still managed to damage his ankle whilst he did it and they had to get a moody doctor to look at it.

The funny thing was, after the alarm went off, so to speak, the coppers couldn't find a picture of Blake in his file at Scotland Yard and that give him a bit more time. Almost all the Sunday papers had been printed and the only one they could eventually get a picture in was the *News of the Screws* but George was long gone by then.

What happened was he had teamed up with Mike Randle and Pat Pottle, two anti-nuclear campaigners who were doing eighteen months apiece, and they agreed to help him. He was also helped by an Irishman Sean Bourke, who got him a walkie-talkie of all things. Although the coppers thought he'd go straight to Germany he stayed in London until nearly Christmas, when Mike

Randle smuggled him out in a van and drove him to Berlin. I think Blake's still in Moscow. Pottle and Randle then went and wrote a book about how they did it. The authorities did nothing and then a year later decided to pros them. It looked like it was one of those open and shut cases but the jury refused to convict. Maybe if they'd prossed them sooner they'd have got a conviction. Anyway when it came to it the pair never got all their royalties from the book. I don't suppose they minded that much.

Of course what with Blake's escape and that of Frank Mitchell and Biggs and John McVicar getting away from a prison escort down in Winchester all happening within a few months of each other, there was bound to be an inquiry and they got Lord Mountbatten, whose wife was in love with Hutch, the nightclub singer, to conduct it. Apart from things like having dog-handlers and links with police stations, one of his recommendations was that there should be better hygiene and living conditions for the cons so they wouldn't want to escape so bad. Nearly forty years on the conditions are probably worse in some nicks.

I've never escaped from anything except the remand home and that was more or less a question of walking out. In fact I only had one serious go after approved school and that was when I was still a kid at Feltham and we tried to get to the wall. All we got was a spanking and a half for our trouble.

I know, though, what it is like to be nicked when you think you are away clear so I suppose I know what it is like to be out and over the wall and then get pulled in. If a Londoner was, say, in Manchester in the old days he'd stick out like a sore thumb if he wasn't out of the town quick. You've got to have transport outside the nick and a place lined up to go to. You feel you want to go back home but that's where the coppers are going to be looking for you first. Then there's always the fear someone's going to bubble you. Look how much of their dough the Train Robbers had to give away just to stay out. And the cleverer the escape the more it must hurt. Take John Kendall for a start. He'd been a member of Billy Tobin's Hole in the Wall Gang, which used lorries to ram warehouses long before people called it ram-raiding, and he'd picked up eight years. He managed to get away when he was being taken to Parkhurst and stayed out nearly two years, but he was finally nicked and they took him to Gartree to do him on other charges for what he'd been up to whilst he was out.

That was when Sidney Draper and him got out in that helicopter on 10 December 1987 but John didn't manage to stay out long. They picked him up in a flat in the King's Road at the end of January along with the man, Andrew Russell, who'd hijacked the helicopter in the first place. He picked up an additional seven whilst Andrew drew a ten. They didn't find Sidney for a long time but, when it came to it, he'd gone back to his old stamping ground in Enfield.

It was the same with Roy Webb, whom they called Rubberbones. He was a great escaper, but although he could get out all right, he never seemed to have the contacts to stay out. He come from the North, Cheshire way, and he'd been in the Coldstream Guards in the war before he was done for damaging a gun. He always said it wasn't his fault and it really soured him. He was forever escaping, and he turned up in London at the end of the war when there was literally thousands of deserters. He did a jeweller's and in a panic hit the man over the head. He got eight years and Flash Jimmy, the man who was with him, got a ten. They both had a birching as well. He got off the Dartmoor train once but he was out only a few days before he was picked up, exhausted. But then he also got off the Moor in 1951, I think it was. He'd dug away at his cell wall with a needle of all things, every night shifting about half a pound of concrete which he washed away the next morning when he slopped out. He managed to get into a tunnel that had been there more or less since the prison had been converted back in Victorian times and which come out only a few yards from the wall. He was away but his real trouble was he didn't have any back-up and, of course, it was only a matter of time before he was caught. He got to London, but he was betrayed by a barrow boy. He'd got a few clothes with him and he tried to sell them. The barrow boy told the coppers and that was that.

He got out of Wandsworth in the 60s and said it was to show he could do it, the screws had been saying it was easy enough to get out of Dartmoor but their place wasn't so simple. Again he was only out a few days. I've no idea what happened to him. Like so many others, he just faded away.

My main thing would have been to try and stay out after an escape. If I'd got clear and I hadn't had things planned in advance than there was a number of people I could go to, friends of the family but who weren't known as such. First off I would have stayed in London and then I'd have gone up North, perhaps even abroad. Don't forget Albert had friends in Paris who'd put me up whilst I was having trouble in Brighton with Harry Rogers down there in the 1960s. I'd stayed in a place of theirs in Pigalle for about a month. It wasn't smart but it was clean and decent and they'd even send a gorgeous girl up to keep me company, as well as give me a lovely present for my boy, Francis, when I left. Of course our lot did the same when one of theirs was in trouble. Jacques Mesrine, a really high-class robber and kidnapper for that matter, who was one of the most wanted men in France back in the 1970s, was hid out in Pallister Road, Barons Court, back in 1978. He was later shot dead back in Paris.

If you could stay out, say, four months then the hue and cry would have died down and things would have been better. Remember, in those days if you could stay out for the whole of the rest of your sentence it was wiped out. You was free.

The time that did for me was when I thought it was all right to come back after the Spot slashing. I was in Ireland and I heard Dido Frett and Ray Rosa had been nicked for doing Johnny Carter. I felt responsible. They'd been helping me with my quarrel with the Carters so I arranged to come back to see what I could do to help them. Little did I know the phone was tapped and there they were waiting for me at London airport. Of course, we'd heard rumours about tapping but we didn't take no notice of them. I phoned Doreen in Brighton to say meet me off the plane and that was what did it. I thought it would be nice to have someone meet me. Right sickener it was. One minute I'm walking about as an ordinary passenger and the next someone calls out 'Frank'. I look up and I don't see light of day for seven years.

It wasn't until George Blake got out that the government really started to pay attention and if he hadn't been a spy then I don't think they'd have thought too much about it. They might have swallowed Frank Mitchell leaving the Moor and John McVicar getting away from the coach at Winchester but this was national security. I met Blake when I was in the hospital at Wormwood Scrubs, getting treatment after I was shot in the leg in Mr Smith's Club. He come over to the hospital wing a couple of times. He was rather austere, as if he was superior to the rest of us, which I suppose in a way he was.

2

Black-marketeering was the thing just at the end and a bit after the war. We really kept things to ourselves but there was a bit of trade with people like the Poles who'd come over here with the Polish Army. It was a couple of them who got nicked over the arrest of a Russian called Reuben

Martirosoff, whom they called Russian Robert. He used to be a big card player in a club called the Bees which I think Italian Jock, Albert's brother, took an interest in.

Martirosoff was found dead one morning at the beginning of November 1945 with his hat over his head on the back seat of a car, an Opel it was, in Chepstow Place, North Kensington. It's smart today but it wasn't then. Someone had shot him through the back of the head. There was blood everywhere, including the steering column. Easy enough, you'd say. All the coppers had to do was match the prints and there it was.

You'd think that the people who did it would have taken his money or whatever and thrown the rest of his stuff away but no. A couple of days later a Pole called Marian Grondkowski was found down the East India Dock Road with Robert's watch and cigarette lighter and his wallet. I know some people get touches of guilt and want to be caught but this man was meant to be a pro. What he then did was grass his mate, Henryk Malinowski. And when they nicked him, in turn he said it was Grondkowski. When it come to the trial each of them said it was the other who had shot Russian Robert and forced him to go along with it. It had been a robbery and they'd got about £150 between them. You might have thought that Grondkowski, the one with the wallet and watch was the one who really did it, but which one had never really mattered. They both swung. But it shows you the dangers of dealing with people who can turn on you. Mostly I, and people like me, dealt with people from approved school or Borstal, or from the neighbourhood who we knew or who someone had vouched for. It was much safer but you couldn't do it all the time.

It was risky being in the black market in the sense of getting rid of the gear. The blag was easy enough but then you was at the mercy of other people. At the end of the war when the black market was at its best, if you got hold of any silk stockings then you was your own master. Them, snout and Scotch were winners and you could ask your own price. Tom was even better because you could carry it around in your pocket.

If I wanted to sell and I hadn't got a buyer lined up I'd go down somewhere like Bobby's Club in Rupert Court off Rupert Street and do a deal. If you was lucky you'd have the gear in a garage but cars weren't all that common and people like us didn't always have garages. You couldn't leave it in the car and so very often it would be in someone's front room. One problem was the nosey-parkers, people who'd look on from behind their curtains. The plus was that they didn't have phones, so if you was seen loading up by some curtain twitcher then chances were you'd be on your way before they could put on a hat and coat and run down the nick. If you'd got the gear in a house then you'd do the deal after dark. The man would come over or send someone with the money, and you'd have someone with you so you could count and load at the same time. What you tried to do was have between five and ten really decent buyers over all London; people whose money was solid. If you couldn't unload it on them then your troubles was just starting.

Of course the police would try and stop you. By the end of the war and just after there was night-time round-ups and I remember in January 1946 they closed all the bridges over the Thames from Hammersmith to Blackfriars in the hope of catching people. It wasn't a great success as I recall. What they was after was the professionals, but all they ended up with was a few people in unlawful possession of petrol.

There had been another raid in Soho the previous month; everyone they could find there and in Mayfair got rounded up. I remember Billy Hill telling me about it. All they got that time was a few deserters. Mind you, Billy was having identity papers and army passes printed by the dozen around then, so I suppose it was a tribute to his work that so few people got done.

You never really needed to go to, say, Leeds unless a place was stuck up for you. It was a long way, petrol was rationed and there was always the chance of a pull. Anyway, there was enough little factories around the back of New Oxford Street to keep you busy. That's where they made women's clothes. Very often there wasn't a burglar alarm at all and they didn't even take very much notice of security. You'd have your Stillsons and clip off the padlock and that was that. If you thought there was a burglar alarm then you'd have a bellman with you. Jock Robinson, who was known as Jock the Fitter, was a good man and Charlie Gibbs was another good bellman. So was Jimmy Ford. He was one who had a bit of bad luck once when he did a job with Albert Baffy in Sloane Square. Albert was nicked straight away but Jimmy, who'd done a bit of boxing as a boy, got clear. He'd been on the run about twenty months when he was recognised by an off-duty copper who'd known him from the boxing. Jim had been a good soldier, very brave. He was at Dunkirk and he picked up a medal.

3

Billy Hill lived in a flat in Moscow Road just off Paddington. Sometimes the chaps would go down the Turkish baths at the Porchester Hall which was just nearby. They've all more or less gone, nowadays, but at one time they was all over London. There was a hotel in Russell Square had one and there were big baths in Jermyn Street. If you was out on the town and missed the last train you could go and sweat the booze off in one of them. You'd have some steam and then be given a straight massage – no question of a hand job or the risk of getting your ring felt – wrapped up for the night in a sheet and next morning you'd get a cup of tea before you left. It wasn't at all expensive either, but I never really fancied them myself.

Whiteleys, the store in Queensway, was a home from home for Eva and her mates. It was considered really posh and they were always at it there. The founder got himself topped on the premises by Horace Rayner, his illegitimate son of all people; same first name as Lawton, although the judge never used it. Anyway Whiteley wouldn't recognise Horace, who was absolutely on his uppers, when in January 1907 he went and got a gun, took it to the store, and demanded his father recognise him as the son and heir and all the loot that went with it. You have to give the old man credit. He wouldn't and Rayner shot his father between the eyes and then turned the gun on himself. He shot himself in the eye and the bullet exited through the cheek and he recovered. It was rather like when I was shot at Turnmills, except that never hit my eye. They found a letter in his pocket saying it was his father who had brought it on himself. The judge thought he was bound to swing but he was wrong.

Public opinion thought Horace had been hard done by and something like 200,000 people signed petitions for his reprieve. It shows what public opinion can do sometimes. He was reprieved but he tried to top himself twice whilst he was in the nick and he wasn't out two years before he died.

People tell me the best Chinese restaurants in London are in Queensway but I don't think I've ever been in one. I was well out from being in one of them back in 1977, when the Wo Sung Wo did for their rivals the Sui Fong. They just turned up with cleavers and swords and three customers got slashed. That was the end of the Sui Fong as the stars of London. It was almost all Wo Sung Wo after that. But they keep themselves mainly to themselves.

4

I suppose the biggest villain in West London was one who was never ever done and that was Peter Rachman, the slum landlord. When he died in 1962 he must have owned near enough 500 properties, from flats to houses to brothels in St Stephens Gardens and round there. He come over after the war and a spell in a Russian labour camp and he started buying up tenanted houses, getting rid of the tenants and letting the properties out again, mainly to West Indians. He wasn't too particular how he got rid of the tenants either. He'd encourage a whole load of West Indians in the next door flat to have all night parties and once he simply had the roof taken off over some people who wouldn't move out of a place in Bayswater. Then he had a whole collection of rent collectors, like Norbert Rondel who'd put the fear of God in you simply by looking at you. Norbert got a few years after he was convicted of biting someone's ear off. He then said he hadn't been properly defended and tried to sue his barrister. He got all the way to the House of Lords but it went against him. It became a famous case in the law reports and he was still trying to get his conviction quashed the last I heard.[1]

Rachman was a friend of both Mandy Rice-Davies and Christine Keeler and he had an affair with Christine. He died when he was 42, and the story is that he'd been humping some girl so hard he collapsed the next day. He was rushed to Edgware General Hospital but he died. He'd got a gold bracelet with all his bank account numbers engraved on the inside. There's another story that he didn't die and the body was switched, so he must be sitting on some island somewhere with JFK and Elvis.

---

[1] Rondel v Worsley. [1969] 1 AC 191.

5

If you're a brief in England you're fairly safe from the chaps unless you start doing business with them. That's what made the disappearance of the solicitor Janice Weston, who lived in Holland Park, back in September 1983 so surprising. She worked for the big firm Charles Russell and when she didn't show on a Monday they raised the alarm. Her body was found up the A1 near St Neots. She'd been badly beaten and the coppers said it was probably with a car jack. Her husband was working in Paris and she'd gone home after doing a bit of overtime on the Saturday. On the table in the flat was her meal not cleared away and she'd left her bag behind. It wasn't sex, because she'd not been assaulted, and it wasn't robbery because her purse was under the driving seat. No one could work out what she was doing up there on a wet Saturday. A few years later there was a story given by a prisoner that she'd been killed by a South London face called 'Chic' Fowler, but if he exists I've never heard of him and no one I've spoken to has either.

It was down at Gloucester Road tube station that someone killed the Polish Countess Lubienska, a very different class from those black marketeers. She'd been a very rich woman and nothing really had gone right for her. Her husband had been killed in the Russian Revolution. Then her son was killed in the Second World War and then she was carted off to Auschwitz. She survived and come to England when, at the end of May 1957, she was stabbed not even late at night, just about 10.15 p.m. as she got out of the train. She died before they could get her to hospital. No one was ever sure who did it. There was one story that it was some Teddy Boys who were around at the time and another that it was political. Sometimes in the nick you heard whispers about who it was did something, but in all the years I was in I never heard a word about her death.

It was funny because a few years before, August 1953 I think it was, there was another case involving a Pole which was never solved either. It wasn't in London but in Bradford and the man was a priest called Henry Borynski. Someone telephoned him, and his housekeeper heard him say he'd go. He just walked out of his home and was never seen again. His housekeeper watched him turn the corner and he just vanished. Never took any money from his bank account either. One story says he went behind the Iron Curtain, but I don't know.

There's always crime at tube stations. There was another over in North London at Finsbury Park in December 1992 when a man, Jonathan Zito, was stabbed in the eye by a schizophrenic, Christopher Clunis. Clunis just went up to him on the platform. He got sent to Rampton and the last I heard he'd started an action against the local council who'd had him in care before the stabbing, saying they shouldn't have released him. I never heard if he got any money. Zito's wife set up a trust to help victims.

In October 1984 Johnny Maile, who was known as Johnny the Flower and who ran a flower stall at Earls Court tube station, was shot dead at his flower stall. He had witnessed Charlie Richardson's arrest after his escape and then he'd given a long account to the papers. There was talk at the time that somehow Charlie had been involved, but I'm pleased to say that at Johnny's inquest the police said there was no truth in the suggestion whatever. They never got no one for that either.

It wasn't exactly a crime, although some people wasn't sure he hadn't been done, but Charlie Taylor, who was a big fraudsman and once was a great mate of Billy Hill's, dropped dead on the tube coming home from giving evidence at the Bailey back in the 1960s. He'd turned grass which goes to show sometimes there is a God after all, like Stinie Morrison said, when he heard one of the coppers who give evidence against him in the case had been killed in an air raid.

One of the most famous cases come in July 1959 just after the police tried to arrest a man at South Kensington tube. It led to a copper being shot dead. What happened was that a German crook, Gunther Podola, broke into the flat of a model and stole some of her jewellery and furs. He also went and took some letters and he thought he could put a bit of black on her. Good for her, she wasn't having any and she called the coppers. They had a trace on her line and the next call came from South Kensington station.

Two coppers were sent to arrest him and, of course, Podola was on his toes. He was chased into a block of flats at 105 Onslow Square. One of the coppers then went in search of help and the other, a Sergeant Ray Purdy, remained on guard. They can't have searched Podola and Purdy must have turned away an instant because he was shot at point-blank range. The other copper was after him at once but they lost him and Podola made his way to the Claremont House Hotel in Queen's Gate where he had a room.

He was traced there and officers broke in. By the time they got him out he was unconscious and after a spell in the nick he was taken to hospital. It's funny. The police was going through a good spell after the killing of PC Summers, but now things turned against them and there was stories that Podola had been beaten up. There'd been a fund set up for Purdy's widow but now the contributions started to dry up.

On anyone's showing Podola was in a mess. There was questions in the House of Commons, because when he come to court he was walking supported by a couple of coppers. There was all sorts of questions being asked, but the Pros said that he'd been behind a door and when that had been knocked down it and a big copper fell on him. Podola had been knocked over a chair and he landed in the fireplace.

Anyway the first thing was that he began saying he couldn't remember a thing about what had happened, and if he genuinely couldn't then he wasn't what they called 'fit to plead'. And if that was right then he couldn't be topped. So they had a jury in to decide if he was faking it. The doctors who saw him was split two each for the Defence and the Pros. In fact it went against him because he went and recognised someone who'd brought him cigarettes in the nick when he was on remand. The jury said he was fit to plead and the second jury had no doubt he'd done it. Topped.

6

It's amazing how things can get out of hand sometimes. When there was a gun battle in Fulham back in February 1968, just a couple of years after the Torture Trial, people was saying how it was a war between scrap metal merchants, but it was nothing of the kind. It had all blown up over Tony Lawrence, who had a site in Waterford Road, not being served after hours in the Queen Elizabeth in Bagley Lane something like two years earlier. He'd got the hump and there'd been a big fight and it all came on top from there on in. Some people were prossed over the fight. Others said they was grasses and should have kept their mouths shut. And then a bomb got thrown into the scrapyard of one of the witnesses. It was after that Tony started buying in weapons and a bit after he got a pull from the police over the bombing. He got the hump even more and it all ended with Tony Lawrence's foreman, Baba Elgar, being shot dead and Tony ending up getting fourteen years at the Bailey for conspiracy to cause a dangerous explosion.

7

Just as legends lived on in prison, so they did in Broadmoor where I ended up. This one was well before my time in 1922. He was Ronald True and there had been a lot of trouble about him not hanging when a young kid swung at the same time. It was always said that he'd been reprieved and sent to Broadmoor because somehow he'd got connections and this kid Henry Jacoby hadn't.

True had been well educated but apparently he'd always been one of those who'd tortured small animals when he was a child. Then he was sent abroad by his family and he learned to fly. He was a conman, really. Took a fellow for a lot of money and was forever passing dud cheques and walking out of hotels leaving the bill. Then he robbed a brass, Olive Young, and took up with a Mrs Wilson, threatening to shoot her if she went out dancing with other men.

One night he just turned up at Olive Young's flat at 13a Finborough Road in Fulham, spent the night with her and clubbed her to death with a rolling pin after he brought her a cup of tea the next morning. The landlady saw him and he give her half a crown as a tip to let the girl sleep on. He can't have been all that mad because he started pawning her jewels. Of course he was nicked in a matter of hours, in a box at the Hammersmith Palace of Varieties where he'd gone for the show. He got convicted but he was reprieved. The doctors said he'd got some mental condition brought on by drug taking and there was also some suggestion he'd got the pox.

He lived on in Broadmoor until he died in 1951 just a few years before I arrived. Even then he was talked about as being the life and soul of the parties they had there. They'd had a concert party, like the end of the pier shows, called the Loonatics or something like that, and he was one of the stars.

You expect streets in Soho or the Gorbals or the East End to have more than one murder take place in them but you don't really expect it in the same street in Fulham. However, in May 1948 in Finborough Road they found the body of another brass, Winifred Mulholland. She'd come down from Durham and had been living in Brixton. There was some story she was going to go to Canada to get married. When they found the body they weren't sure if she'd just fallen off a balcony, or if someone had tried to make it look that way, and then they decided on the second. After that it wasn't too difficult to work out it was a man called George Epton who lived in a flat just near where she was found. At first he said he'd never seen the woman but what he'd done was beaten her with a hammer and a flat-iron for good measure. Later he said he'd picked her up in Piccadilly and taken her home for dinner. Then he'd missed £9 from his pocket and beaten her up when first she said she hadn't taken it and then he'd seen it by her shoes. He said he only used his fist and after he'd given her a couple of blows he then went to sleep and when he woke up found out she was dead. He was another who kept the body for a bit and then tipped it over the balcony. He was lucky and all. They were still talking about stopping the death penalty at the time and he got reprieved.

8

If there's a killing or a failed attempt it's never really squared up. Maybe if something goes on top in a pub or a club, spur of the moment sort of thing, well that's one thing but otherwise it's not forgotten. There's always going to be repercussions even if it takes years. It's no different from them Corsican vendettas in Paris just after the war. Things can run twenty years. If you've got a very strong man such as Billy Hill, well sometimes if he was dealing with minor villains he could call things to order. But not with the big boys.

When I think of it Peter Hennessey's a good example. In fact, he caused so much trouble over the years – even though he didn't know it and he didn't mean to. It went on all over South East London, Kensington and ended up back in South East London again. He was the one who was having that straightener with Eddie Richardson in Mr Smith's Club when Dickie Hart started shooting and I ended up on the murder charge. That started a chain of events which brought down poor Charlie Richardson and ended with me having a twenty.

Then when Peter was at the Royal Garden Hotel in High Street, Kensington, for a boxing evening, he gets a bit drunk and he begins causing all sorts of trouble. He was trying to start a whip for some charity of his own which wasn't the charity of the evening and he ends up dead on the floor, stabbed 60 times. Paddy O'Nione, who was known as Paddy Onions, was meant to have been the one who stabbed him, him and Jimmy Coleman who was related to the Arifs were put on trial. I'm pleased to say they was chucked. But things didn't end there.

Paddy Onions had done a good bit of work with me over the years. He was with us in Manchester when we did a tie-up job on Mrs Post and also in that job with the Gibbs brothers in Bedford when I was done. Paddy's mother was with Jock Robinson, Jock the Fitter. Anyway Paddy gets shot in November 1982 outside a wine bar his son owned in the Tower Bridge Road. Someone had had a go at him a few months earlier and shot him in the face but he'd survived.

Then the man who was said to have done him for five grand died in a police cell. He'd been in Parkhurst with Peter's brother Mickey and he was a wild man. He was going under the name Jimmy Davey but his real name was

Bowman. He'd had a brother who was killed and that was when he'd changed it. Earlier Jimmy had done a six for cutting a copper. Anyway he was arrested in Coventry and when the coppers come to take him back for questioning over Paddy they say he lunged at one of them. He was put in a choke-hold and he lost consciousness and the doctors switched the machine off a couple of weeks later.

It was in the Ranelagh Yacht Club in Fulham that Johnny Bindon stabbed Johnny Darke to death in November 1978. This Darke wasn't related to the good fellow who was a friend of Mickey Green but a man who'd been a grass for years. I'm glad to say the jury ruled it was self-defence. A solicitor come to see me in the nick about giving evidence of what Darke was like but they never called me, which was just as well. In none of the cases where I've given evidence for anybody has it worked out well. John did better than having me give evidence, he had the actor Bob Hoskins tell the court what a good guy he was.

John was a good actor. He was in that film *Poor Cow* which was such a success and in lots of TV series but he went on the river and become unreliable. Women thought the world of him, though, and he lived with the model Vicky Hodge for years. They say he could hang a few beer glasses – half pint ones, mind – on his thin and thick. I never saw him do the trick myself. In the end though he got AIDS. It seems so long since he died; October 1993 it was. I went to the funeral, of course.

9

It was down in King Street in Hammersmith that the Welsh girl, Elizabeth Jones, got picked up for the killing of a taxi-driver, George Heath, who'd been found shot at the beginning of October 1944 on the Great West Road, near Staines. Someone first found a wallet and took it to the local nick, and then about an hour later another geezer found the body. The man had been shot in the back. He was a driver for a car hire firm and his Ford saloon was missing. It wasn't Brain of Britain work to reckon that if you found the car you'd be close to finding who killed him and the car turned up in Lurgan Avenue which is just off the Fulham Palace Road, funnily enough not far from where Virgin Publishing's got their offices. Three days later a copper on his beat found it and then it was a question of waiting to see who came near it. The man who did was a US army deserter called Karl Hulten. When they nicked him he'd got an automatic pistol with him, and at first he said he was an officer in one of their parachute regiments. It shows how bright he was. He gave his correct regiment – not that it would have taken long to find out – just promoted himself. Then he give varying stories about how he'd got the car and finally he said he'd been with a girl called Georgina Grayson, so he went and took the coppers to where he said she lived in King Street.

Georgina turned out to be Elizabeth Jones. She said she was a cabaret artiste but really what she did was a bit of strip-tease, funnily enough in the Blue Lagoon in Carnaby Street where that Margaret Cook (see Chapter 2) worked. They had her in and released her but then she met up with a man who was a War Reserve copper, and she said if he'd seen what she'd seen he wouldn't be able to sleep at night. Then it all fell out.

Hulten had told her he was a Chicago gangster when she met him at a coffee stall in Hammersmith and they went on a four-day spree of nicking cars and doing a bit of blagging. He went and knocked a girl cyclist off her bike and stole her money and then he told Jones he wanted to rob a taxi-driver, because I suppose he thought the man would have more money than the girl he'd done. In the meantime they done another girl – hit her over the head with an iron bar and got five shillings. Big time.

It was after that they flagged down Heath and got him to take them down the Great West Road to where the Chiswick flyover is now. The driver was boosting his price, because he'd wanted ten bob for a short ride when he'd seen a man in American uniform. He must have thought he was a soft touch. It was down the road that Hulten shot Heath and the girl took over the driving.

When it came to the trial they went against each other. She'd written him a letter from Holloway, blaming him and saying he'd forced her to go through Heath's pockets, which the authorities intercepted, and that really did for him. It didn't help her much because he tried to put the blame equally on her. She got a recommendation for mercy but of course they was both sentenced to hang. Eva was in Holloway at the same time as her, doing six months for hoisting.

It was a big thing. For a start it was about the biggest trial at the Old Bailey since the war had begun and a lot of women didn't have much time for the girl. There was even one factory in Scotland which threatened to strike if she didn't swing, which wasn't going to do much for the war effort. She got reprieved eventually but he swung. I read somewhere once that Winston Churchill, who was the prime minister then, thought it was wrong and she should have been topped as well. A few years ago they made a film about the case.

George Sewell, the father of the actor, always fancied himself as having sort of stood back to back with Darby Sabini. He liked to be known as the Cobblestone Kid and he was a receiver and a grass as well. He give evidence against Jimmy O'Connor, who was known as Ginger, when Ginger was done for the murder of a coal merchant in Hampton Road, Kilburn, in 1941 in a robbery which went wrong. He said Ginger had sold him some tom which came from the robbery. Ginger swore he hadn't, but he still come within an ace of being topped. The authorities must have had some doubt because he was reprieved the night before he was due to go. Later, Ginger went and married the brief, Nemone Lethbridge, and for a time he did well writing plays. He come out of North Wharf Road, Paddington, which itself wasn't the best bit of a very bad area.

10

The Towpath murders in 1974 were the ones which created the biggest stir in West London and it was one of them cases that, because the authorities never released the name of who they suspected, there's been so much speculation that it was a very famous boxer. Personally I've never believed it was, but that's the trouble. If people don't say what's what then rumours are bound to fly and they hurt innocent people.

Whoever done them became known as Jack the Stripper; after Jack the Ripper, of course. This was a bit clever because most of the girls were found naked and, if they did have the right man, because he worked in a paint-stripping business. The first girl was a thirty-year-old brass called Hannah Tailford, who went under a number of names. She turned up on 2 February 1974 in the Thames near Hammersmith Bridge. Most of her clothes were missing but her stockings were still around her ankles. She'd got bruising on her face and her knickers were stuffed in her mouth.

Hannah seems to have been mixed up in the porn business. Although she lived in South Norwood, she worked out of a flat in Victoria and when the police looked there it had studio lighting equipment and a camera. Most brasses who aren't actually on the street keep a book with the names and telephone numbers of their punters – the black book they call it, maybe after black for blackmail

– and that was gone. So the police thought it might have been a client who'd done her to stop her leaning on him. Funnily enough, though, when it came to an inquest there was an open verdict and since there was no evidence to show that she was murdered the police didn't go on treating it as a crime. That was despite there having been another brass done in the area in the meantime.

This time it was at Duke's Meadow. You hear it on the television when they're having the Boat Race 'Oxford is leading as they come to . . .' The new girl was Irene Lockwood and she had been strangled. Again the police thought she might have been blackmailing her former punters. She'd provided the alibi for a man accused, a year earlier, of murdering another brass, Vicki Pender.[2]

Then the body of a third brass turned up when Helen Barthelemy was found a couple of weeks later, a little way from the river in a driveway near Swincombe Avenue in Brentford. She used to hang around the Jazz Club, in Westbourne Grove, which had a big black clientele. Four of her teeth were missing and she had traces of paint spray on her body – which made the police think it might have been kept in a paint-strip shop before being dumped. There was traces of sperm in her mouth and they worked out she had either been orally raped or that she had plated the man before she died. Now they reckon that if one man was responsible for the murders the blackmail theory was wrong.

The next day the coppers must have thought their Sundays had all come at once when Kenneth Archibald, a caretaker, walked into Notting Hill police station and confessed to killing Irene Lockwood. He worked in a club

[2] On 2 July 1963 Colin Welt Fisher received life imprisonment for the murder of Vicki Pender at her flat in Adolphus Road, Finsbury Park, on 19 March 1963. The prosecution alleged both had been taking drugs.

for Joey Cannon of the big Notting Hill family. There were some good men amongst them but Joey was a toe rag and a grass. After the fight in Frith Street he'd been hired by Spot to shoot Albert and Hilly, but I'd taken the gun off him and explained the facts of life. Then he was meant to be the bodyguard to Spot, but he wasn't there the night I did Jack outside Hyde Park Mansions. Just as well, it was probably the best day's work he didn't do in his life. He was the one whose eye I tried to put out in Pentonville.

Anyway Archibald fitted the bill. He told the coppers he must have lost his temper and strangled her. Then he'd taken her clothes off and rolled her into the river. He'd taken the clothes home and burned them. Unfortunately there was no way they could tie him to the murders of either Tailford or Barthelemy so that theory went out the window.

They put Archibald on trial at the Bailey for just Lockwood's murder. Of course, at the trial he took his confession back and luckily for him the jury believed him. They was only out 40 minutes. Just as well for him since he didn't do it. What seems to have happened was that there'd been a break-in at the club and he thought he had been in the frame. He'd gone and drunk six pints of beer before he walked into the police station and made this moody confession.

It was funny, though, that whilst Archibald was in custody the murders stopped. It was as if the killer knew what he was doing and wanted the blame to fall on someone else. Maybe the brasses were just being a bit more careful in their choice of clients, but I can't believe that's right. Most of this lot weren't what you might call quality and they'd need to take what was going. The next murder come on 14 July when Mary Fleming, a mother of two, was found in a sitting position near a garage in Berrymead Road, Chiswick. She too was naked and her denture was missing. Again, someone had come in her mouth and traces of paint spray were on her body.

The next one turned up in the November, when Margaret McGowan was discovered on a pile of rubble in a car park in Hornton Street near Kensington High Street. Again spots of paint covered her body and she had a tooth missing. She'd been missing a month. The last of the killings was discovered in the middle of February the next year, when the body of Bridie O'Hara was found behind a store-shed off Westfield Road, Acton.

There was links between all the killings and the police went back to the theory that it had to be one man. The girls was all small and they all worked the Bayswater-Kensington beat. The scientists could tell from marks on their bodies that they'd all been suffocated before their clothes was taken, and they was convinced the girls were kept in a store before their bodies were left out to be found. Finally all were found in or near the Thames.

The coppers managed to trace the paint on the bodies to a covered transformer near to a paint-spray shop on the Heron Factory Estate in Acton. Whilst they were still working on the 7,000 odd people who were employed on the estate in June 1965 a married man from South London topped himself, leaving a note saying that he was unable to stand the strain any longer.

What is certain is that the killings stopped and the police put it about that this man was in fact Jack the Stripper. Then the rumours started, because it was about this time that the boxer Freddie Mills topped himself or got took out in Goslett Yard, a little turning off the Charing Cross Road near where the Astoria is, and just round the corner from where Freddie had a sort of Chinese restaurant club. There was all sorts of stories about that. Some people said he did himself because the place wasn't doing well; that he was half gay and couldn't cope; that he was upset because he wasn't being used as a commentator for boxing on the radio no more; that he was being leaned on for protection and wouldn't pay, or that the Twins did him or that the Chinese Triads did him. Pick any theory you want.

Then there was the story that he was the Stripper. The tale went that some coppers knew it and told him he had to top himself because they didn't want to have anyone arrest him. That's the story that's grown up, and despite the fact that it all happened near enough 40 years ago it has never really gone away.

There was another view that the Stripper was an ex-copper who was a heavy drinker. The story went that he was married but had always fancied brasses. He'd taken up drinking when he wanted to go to the plain-clothes division and they wouldn't let him, so he'd resigned. But who knows?

There was a funny killing just nearby in Ealing. You don't get too many done with crossbows but Diana Maw had a six-inch crossbow bolt in her head when they found her body on the landing outside her flat at Stanley Court in Woodfield Road in July 1988. At first the coppers thought she had been shot by a mugger, but then it emerged that she'd been stalked by her killer for the previous six weeks. There was a photofit issued of a man but then the coppers changed tack and a woman interior designer, who'd been a former girlfriend of Diana's bloke, was charged. There really wasn't any evidence – something like a single witness and you know how chancy that can be. The Pros said the woman was obsessed but when it come to it they offered no evidence against her.

The only other crossbow murder that I can think of offhand was that girl, Debbie Lee Parsons, who got done over in North London back in June 1990. She'd been working in a sauna and, that evening, had meant to go over to help out her boyfriend who had a restaurant. She never turned up and when they found her in Epping Forest she'd been done with a crossbow. They never nicked anyone. One suggestion was she'd been trying to put the black on some serious people, but once again, who knows?

11

Paddington had some big families and some good clubs and it was here that Jack Spot thought he might pitch up and open a club or two after him and his wife Rita put me and the others away for slashing him. He got it wrong. Firstly, Billy Hill had taken up with Gypsy Reilly and she was done in March 1957 for trying to put a man's eye out in the Miramar Club, in the basement of the Miramar Hotel in Paddington, which was really Spot territory. What was she doing over there in the first place? It was Hilly just letting Spot know he was around. She got acquitted. It was one of Patrick Marrinan's last defences before he got thrown out from being a barrister because of his association with Billy.

Then Rita goes into the Market Club in Shepherd's Bush and some people take objection to her being let in. The club gets busted up. After that in June 1958 Spot opens up the Highball in Lancaster Gate on the money Rita's made from selling her life story, but that got done over badly the next month. And a month after that it was burned down. And that was it for Spot – he was off to Ireland.

There was some seriously tough clubs up in Notting Dale. There was one run by Ernest Bell. Him and his sons fell out with another local family, the Smiths. The feud was another which ran for years and in May 1960 James Smith got shot. The end result was that Ernest Bell's son, Ernest junior, and a neighbour picked up seven and five respectively for manslaughter.

The most curious of all those clubs in West London was the Celebrity at 10 Ruston Close. It was run by Charlie

Brown – no connection with the man who had the Railway down the East End to my knowledge. Charlie was the doorman of a club in Kingley Street in Soho and when it shut down for the night he'd send the punters to the Celebrity. What the punters didn't know was that 10 Ruston Close was really 10 Rillington Place, where John Reginald Halliday Christie had murdered all those women back in the 1940s. The club got raided and there they all were in the room where Christie had done the girls. It got closed and I think the whole place was torn down and rebuilt without No 10. The other story about Christie is that apparently the pathologist who did the post mortem of someone who had been topped was allowed to keep bits and pieces of him for medical research, and the one who did Christie kept his orchestras for his students to work on. Not that much different from keeping the kids' parts, like these hospitals have done, when you think about it. Even murderers usually have families.

Before the place got torn down, though, people had been paying half a crown to see the rooms where the bodies were, and someone was done for nicking the door handle of the place.

Keeping the bits reminds me of that dog, the prison governor Lawton, after Harryboy Jenkins had been hanged for de Antiquis (see Chapter 4). He wouldn't return Harryboy's clothes, saying he'd been topped in them but here were the buttons, braces and shoelaces which they'd taken away in case he'd harmed himself and cheated everyone out of their fun. It was rather like that case long ago when a man hanged himself in a cell in Sunderland. The widow wanted his clothes but the Poor Law Guardians said they were entitled to them. Eventually the Home Secretary was brought in and he told the magistrates they had to give the widow back the clothes, less the cost of the application and postage.

12

I see that Bert Wickstead died in March this year. He'd been a Commander at the Yard. I never come across him myself, but I knew scores who did and they included some very good men such as the Tibbs family and Alan and George Dixon, Reggie Dudley and Bobby Maynard. He was reckoned to be just about the King of the Verbal. When Reggie and Bobby got done for that Epping Torso Murder, when Billy Mosley got cut up and Mickey Cornwall got killed as well, Wickstead was asked by a defence brief if he had a tape recorder when he was interviewing the men. He said he did. Then when he was asked why he didn't have it on, he replied he was a police officer and police officers didn't use tape recorders.

I was never verballed too bad but it was what your barrister was terrified of, and nine times out of ten there wasn't anything you could do about it. What you'd have was a trial within a trial, with the jury out of the room to see if you could get the evidence ruled inadmissible. The judge would listen to what the coppers had to say about how you'd come to make these remarks which did for you. The coppers would say how they'd written down the answers not at the time but at the earliest opportunity, and that could be up to nine hours later in the canteen. Then they'd be asked if their colleague had helped them recollect and they'd say it was completely independent. After that they'd be asked how the reports were word for word the same and the judge would interrupt and say 'That's because they've remembered accurately'. They could have been interviewing you for hours and the questions and answers, when they was read out, took about five minutes at most. Why was that then? That was because they'd only written things down which was relevant. Later on, when they got a bit more savvy and sussed no one was believing them, the coppers would agree they'd compiled their notes together in the canteen, but said they'd only been refreshing each other's memories.

Of course nine hundred and ninety-nine times out of a thousand the judge would let the evidence in. You got a second bite at the cherry because the jury would come back in and you'd go through it all again and sometimes, thank the Lord, they'd think the coppers had made it up. I could never understand how people believed that serious and experienced men like me and others would start to confess the moment we got to the nick. Or we'd make some damaging remark on the way in the car and then say nothing at the station. That dog Lawton said once in a judgement that it was not surprising that men like us would want to unburden themselves. Something like that.

One of the most famous cases over verbals was that case of Whiteway who murdered a couple of girls – he'd been a family friend of one of them – on the towpath down at Teddington. He was done by that copper Herbert Hannam and it was always thought he'd verballed him up rotten. Two teenage girls were found raped and murdered at the end of May 1955. I think some of the old-time coppers got a kick out of being in the witness box and fencing off the briefs' questions. It's like, if they'd come from different circumstances, they'd have been briefs themselves and Hannam was one of them.

What happened was that Whiteway signed a confession and then denied it. What else was he to do, and old Peter Rawlinson, who was later Lord Rawlinson, put Hannam through the paces about how he'd got the confession out of the man. It was the first time any brief had ever done it to a copper, with that much success anyway, and he did open up gaps in Hannam. Even some other coppers thought Hannam had been pushing it too far, but the jury wouldn't have it that it was totally manufactured and they weren't out 50 minutes. After that there was a bit of an outcry, with the public writing in and saying it was wrong to make these attacks on coppers.

It took years before the public realised that coppers made things up. What was so wrong was that people who'd defended you and knew what was going on just turned a blind eye when they got on the bench a couple of years later. They were the ones who could have put a stop to things if they'd wanted.

13

I suppose the murder which had so much to do with West London, even though it didn't take place there, and which has lived on in people's memories is the Hanratty case. It's funny how so few cases are known by the victim's names. You think of Heath, Cream, Craig and Bentley, Hanratty or even the place where it happened, but you don't often know of the other way around, certainly not if the fellow was caught. I suppose the Hulton and Jones case was known as the Cleft Chin Murder because the taxi-driver had a cleft chin, but who knows his name?

The reason it's so tied in to West London is that it was at the Vienna Hotel in Sutherland Avenue, Maida Vale, that Peter Alphon wa staying on the night of the killing. He was the first person picked up for the murder of Michael Gregsten and the rape of Valerie Storie, his girlfriend, back in August 1961. It's also the area where the characters who put Hanratty away come from. Whoever done the killing picked the pair up when they was in a car parked up at Dorney Reach near Slough. He made them drive around and eventually shot Gregsten at a place called Deadman's Hill on the A6 and then he raped the girl and shot her, paralysing her.

The car was found abandoned in Ilford and they had an Identikit out in no time. A landlord in Finsbury Park said it looked like a man staying there. It turned out to be Alphon, who'd booked in there the night after the murder. When the coppers questioned him he said he'd been in the Vienna. The police took a statement from him and let him go. There was no things like police bail then.

Then the gun turns up down the seat of a No 36A bus and the next thing that happens is that the manageress of the Vienna finds a couple of cartridge cases in a chair in Room 24 which link up. Then the manager on the night of the killing, a man called Nudds – well that was one of his names – who'd been given the hoof by now, said that Alphon had been out late on the night of the killing and was looking nervous when he saw him the next morning. The trouble was that Alphon had been in Room 6. The fellow who'd been in 24 had signed in as J. Ryan, which was a name that Hanratty used. Then what does Hanratty do but ring up the copper in charge and say he was in Liverpool, but he's not coming in because he's wanted for housebreaking.

He got nicked in Blackpool and Valerie Storie picks him out on an ID parade. She'd already got it wrong when Alphon had stood on one earlier. There was also a prison grass who said Hanratty had confessed. I know the Pros used to use them more in those days, when juries didn't know any better, but even so they must have realised they had a weak case. However, Hanratty's alibi went belly up, and even though well into the trial he said he was in Rhyl – and in fact it looked as though he could have been – it didn't do him no good.

Over the years people have been on to Alphon to say he done it, and from time to time he half says he's done it and then he goes and says he hasn't.[3] One of his stories was that he and Charles France, who was meant to be a friend

---

[3] See for example the *Sunday Times*, 14 May 1967.

of Hanratty's, had framed him. Charles was the one who told the police about Hanratty saying that shoving things down the back of a bus seat was the way to hide stolen tom. The Pros made a lot of it but you'd think every jewel thief would know about that. France had been the manager of the Rehearsal Club in Archer Street, but he'd got the sack and was making a few bob marking at the snooker club under Jack Solomon's offices. He topped himself between the verdict and Hanratty being hanged. He left a number of letters but the authorities have never released them.

Hanratty's friends and family have always fought and fought to get his name cleared and just about every piece of evidence for the Pros has been discredited in one way or another. But the DNA test put paid to that – it looks as though it may have been Hanratty after all.

POSTSCRIPT

It's easy to mock when we say things were different when Billy Hill and Jack Spot and Reggie and Ronnie – and Charlie and Eddie for that matter – were about, but women were safer on the streets in those days. I can't say there weren't fights in dance halls but we didn't go into places and just fire into the crowd, or hold them all up as some of the Yardies have been doing. And we certainly didn't go into restaurants and pull rings off women's fingers while they were having their meals, like what happened in Knightsbridge earlier this year.

I don't suppose there'll ever again be as big gangland funerals as there were for Ronnie, Charlie and then Reggie. They were the ones in the limelight, even thirty years later, no matter what Melford Stevenson, the judge, had said about everyone being tired of them.

I can't think how many funerals I've been to in the last few years. And there's plenty I've missed through being away. Billy Blythe – God rest his soul – who died in the nick after he was sent down with me over the Jack Spot slashing, was one. That was big. And, of course, I missed Spot's too, although that was a quiet one. He was as clever as always and didn't want any publicity or anything. No one really ever heard when Spot died. In fact I was in a taxi the other day and the driver told me he knew he was alive. It would be difficult to look up his death because he had so many names: Comaco, Comacho, Comer, Spot, where do you start? From what I've been told, though, he went a few years ago. Buster Edwards and Charlie Wilson from the Train are in the cemetery in Streatham and, like I've said, Tony Ash is in Camberwell New Cemetery. So is

Freddie Mills and George Cornell . . . Jimmy Moody is in the cemetery down in Manor Park. Tommy Smithson, who got shot after he was leaning on some Maltese, is buried in there as well. The Twins and Charlie are all in Chingford Mount. Albert's over in Bromley.

My poor niece Shirley died this summer. She had a brain haemorrhage. She never really got over the time when she was at home in bed and her boyfriend Michael Bowden brought a head on a tray in her room. He and another couple of mates had killed a sort of dosser and then cut him up.

She had a lovely funeral. A lot of the Brindles were there of course. They're a great family. And, what a lovely thing, when the hearse went down the Walworth Road her daughters got out of the car following and walked beside their mother. It was really emotional.

I don't think a lot about death. I'm a practical person, you know it's going to happen, especially at my age, and when it does, it does. Despite all the headaches I've enjoyed my life. I'm quite satisfied. I wouldn't have wanted to be a straight person. I don't frown on people who are; it's just me.

I don't think there's any chance I'll go back to the Roman Catholic Church. It breaks my heart to say it, but you've got to be practical. I might turn people against me by saying this, but when I was a kid Heaven was a big thing up in the clouds you sort of got to by an invisible ladder. Now it's becoming conclusively clear that there isn't anything up there. The Church doesn't talk as much about a real Heaven nowadays. It's all Spirit. If there is a Hell down there, I'll have the chief stoker's job.

As for me, I don't want a big funeral. Otherwise genuine people who may not have a lot of dough at the time may think they've got to send expensive flowers or take half a day off work to come. I'd want to be cremated; end of story. After all I'm not going to be alive to enjoy it. Just having a big funeral is not going to bring me back.

BIBLIOGRAPHY

More about a number of the cases and people mentioned by Frank Fraser can be found in his previous books *Mad Frank* and *Mad Frank's Friends* (Warner Books) and *Mad Frank's Diary* (Virgin Publishing). There is an overview of crime in London in the last century and more particularly in East London in James Morton's *Gangland* and *East End Gangland* (Warner Books). Duncan Campbell provides an overall survey in *The Underworld* (BBC Books).

Duncan Webb's exposures of London's vice, the Messinas and their successors which first appeared in the *Sunday People* can be found in *Line Up for Crime* (Frederick Muller). There are any number of books on the Kray twins, including several by themselves and their brother Charlie. The most comprehensive is John Pearson's *The Profession of Violence* (Penguin Books). Tony Parker wrote an account of the Richardsons in *Rough Justice* (Fontana).

A number of police officers mentioned by Frank Fraser published their memoirs. They include Edward Greeno, *War on the Underworld* (John Long), Leonard Read, *Nipper* (Little, Brown) and John DuRose who deals particularly with the Jack the Stripper or the Towpath murders in *Murder was my Business* (W. H. Allen).

Even before the current fashion for the memoirs of former criminals, Billy Hill wrote *Boss of Britain's Underworld* (the Naldrett Press) and the American pulp writer Hank Jansen wrote his rival's memoirs, *Jack Spot − Man of a Thousand Cuts* (Alexander Moring). Both are extremely difficult to find. Ruby Sparks produced *Burglar to the Nobility* (Arthur Barker). More recently, Peter Scott wrote *Gentleman Thief* (Harper Collins).

There are detailed accounts of some cases including Robert Hancock, *Ruth Ellis* (Weidenfeld Paperbacks). In 1974 Brian McConnell wrote *Found Naked and Dead* (New English Library), also about the Towpath Murders. Leonard Read also deals with the investigation into the death of Freddie Mills. Jack Birtley wrote the biography *Freddie Mills* (New English Library) and Tony Van den Bergh offers a novel suggestion about his death in *Who Killed Freddie Mills?* (New English Library). Paul Foot's *Who Killed Hanratty?* (Jonathan Cape) is the definitive account of the case, whilst Bob Woffinden provides an excellent summary in *Miscarriages of Justice* (Hodder & Stoughton) and also deals with the case of Bobby Maynard and Reggie Dudley. This case is not mentioned by Bert Wickstead in his *Gangbuster* (Macdonalds) but he does deal with the Pen Club case.

The jewel theft from Hatton Garden to which Fraser refers can be found in Christmas Humphrey's *The Great Pearl Robbery of 1913* (Heinemann). For those really interested, the papers on the case and Grizzard's activities generally are stored in the Public Records Office in Kew under reference MEPO 3 236 B. Valerio Viccei wrote his own account of the safe deposit and other raids in *Knightsbridge: The Robbery of the Century* (Blake).

The story of Harold Davidson, the Rector of Stiffkey – pronounced Stukey which rather spoils things – can be found in Christine Keeler's *Sex Scandals*, which quotes extensively from Tom Cullen's fuller version *The Prostitute's Padre*. Shirley Green wrote *Rachman* (Michael Joseph).

As for prison escapes generally, J. P. Bean has most of the more interesting ones in his *Over the Wall* (Headline) and Martin Randle and Pat Pottle retell their involvement in *The Blake Escape* (Harrap).

INDEX